BENEATH *the* TRANSACTION

DISCOVER THE 7 CONDITIONS
THAT TRANSFORM LIFE AND LEADERSHIP

Rooted in Indigenous Wisdom and Modern Leadership

CHRIS PINEDA, PHD

Published by Maison Vero
3002 Dow Avenue,
Suite 112 Tustin, CA 92780

Inquiries may be directed to: Maison Vero, 3002 Dow Avenue, Suite 112 Tustin, CA 92780, or info@graymilleragency.com.

For information about special discounts for bulk purchases, please call 1-949-333-4872 or email info@graymilleragency.com.

Maison Vero is a partner brand of The Gray + Miller Agency, a speaking, literary, and talent consortium.

For more information on the talent represented by The Gray + Miller Agency, or to bring any of our thought leaders to your organization or live event please visit our website at graymilleragency.com

Cover Design: Mike Elwell
Book Design: Mel Wise
Photographer: Tay Steele

Manufactured in the United States of America

Paperback: 978-1-969508-28-8   E-book: 978-1-969508-30-1
Hardcover: 978-1-969508-29-5

Real transformation requires intentionality. I've learned throughout my life that sometimes the most subtle truths carry the greatest wisdom, and this book is full of them.

What makes it even more powerful is that it's written by someone who lives it. Chris is one of the most genuinely kind, humble, and thoughtful people I know. He doesn't just teach these principles, he embodies them.

Whether you're a parent, leader, coach, or just someone who wants to become better and help others do the same, this will both challenge you and equip you. It's practical, deeply human, and it works.

—Colby Bauer, CEO and co-founder of Thread and Carry On

I have had the privilege of working alongside Chris in Hawaii, Oregon, and Wisconsin, and I have witnessed firsthand the kind of transformation he writes about on these pages. What moves me most is his reverence for Indigenous wisdom, not as a mere metaphor, but as foundation. As a Māori, I recognize in his work the enduring truths our ancestors carried: transformation begins in relationship, in the Vā, the sacred relational space between each of us, and in the sharing of HĀ, the breath of life that affirms our shared humanity. Chris challenges the transactional instincts of modern leadership and calls us back to something far older and more enduring. These are lived practices grounded in community and I am honored to endorse it.

—Seamus Fitzgerald, Ngāti Kahungunu-ki-Wairarapa; director of global corporate culture at dōTERRA International

I've read many leadership books over the years, but this one stayed with me. It doesn't simply discuss leading teams—it speaks to the courage required to build real trust. Navigating workplace relationships can be complex and, at times, isolating. This book helped me recognize that sustainable leadership is grounded in shared purpose, vulnerability, consistency, commitment, and a common language that aligns people beyond tasks. More importantly, it gave me permission to be vulnerable with my own team—and in doing so, to lead with greater authenticity and trust. It reminded me that trust isn't a byproduct of leadership, it is the foundation of it. This is the kind of book that invites you to lead differently—and better.

—Maria Lopez Vento, foundation executive

Through powerful storytelling and a practical framework for transformation, Beneath the Transaction challenges readers to move beyond surface-level change. If you're serious about strengthening teams, developing leaders, or rebuilding the social fabric of a community, this is a timely and usable guide. I highly recommend it!

—Brandon A. Wigley, JD, Bader Philanthropies, Inc.

*Many organizations settle for transactional leadership and then wonder why trans-
formation never arrives. In* Beneath the Transaction, *Chris exposes that gap with
clarity and compassion. His invitation to move from the "handshake" to the "breath
of life" mirrors what I have witnessed for decades: joy and purpose are born when we
treat people as human beings, not functions. This book is not just about leadership—it
is about reclaiming the sacred space between us. Read it slowly. Practice it intentionally.
Transformation will follow.*

—Richard Sheridan, CEO, founder, and chief storyteller at Menlo Innovations;
author of *Joy, Inc.: How We Built a Workplace People Love* and *Chief Joy Officer:
How Great Leaders Elevate Human Energy and Eliminate Fear*

*This book is a game changer. For years of coaching at the collegiate and professional
levels and building elite clubs as an entrepreneur, I've learned that success always comes
back to people.* Beneath the Transaction *puts language to that truth. This book will
challenge you to think differently and improve how you connect, lead, and show up for
others. Coach, players, and leaders alike can benefit from this book.*

—Mark Davis, head coach of SLCC Soccer and Utah United

Beneath the Transaction *bridges Indigenous wisdom with practical leadership in a way
that feels both grounded and deeply human. What resonated most for me is how clearly
Chris puts language and structure around what I instinctively knew to be true in my own
business journey: connection, trust, and presence drive results beyond strategy alone. This
framework makes relational leadership intentional, repeatable, and powerful, not just in
organizations, but in personal relationships as well.*

—Evann Walters, CEO of Fresh n' Local Foods

Beneath the Transaction *is a powerful reclamation of relational space. What sets this
work apart is its focus on Vā, the sacred "space between," as the foundation for leadership
and transformation. Instead of providing us with another performance-driven model,
Chris invites us beneath the surface of transactions into the deeper relational field where
identity, belonging, and responsibility are formed. This aligns with what Indigenous
peace-building traditions have long recognized: transformation does not begin with strategy but with the restoration of relationship. By embedding Kapwa, Unggno, and Culture
of One in modern organizational life, he bridges ancestral wisdom and contemporary
leadership in a manner that is both practical and profound. It is not change management;
it is relational reorientation. In a world so full of technique, this book calls us back to
presence, breath, and the courage to honor the Vā.*

—Michael Fusi Ligaliga, PhD; founder of HIVĀ ADR;
associate professor at BYU-Hawaii

For Makenzie—who keeps choosing with me.

Table of Contents

PREFACE

The purpose of this book stands on a simple belief: transformation is possible in your life and in your leadership.

Life, in this context, extends beyond your internal sense of self to include your relationships with family and friends. Leadership extends into your place of work, whether or not you hold a formal title. We all have influence. And your community—your neighborhoods, organizations, and systems—is inseparable from both your life and your leadership.

Across all these contexts runs a common thread: *transaction.*

Transaction shapes how we greet one another, how we communicate, how we govern relationships, and how we structure families, teams, organizations, and communities. Transaction makes the world go round. It is efficient, predictable, and often necessary. Throughout this book, we will explore what transaction looks like in everyday life.

But transaction is also the enemy of transformation.

Transformation, however you define it in this moment, is inherently desired. We want to become. Becoming is part of existence itself, and the moment we stop becoming, we begin to die—perhaps not physically, but emotionally, spiritually, and mentally. Transaction can rob us of self-discovery, deeper meaning, healthier relationships, and purpose-driven action.

Transformation is the process of becoming—specifically, fundamentally shifting toward our positive potential.

As you begin this book, I invite you to consider what you have become and what you are becoming. The more intentional you are in that process, the more likely you are to experience transformation. My hope is that as you read, something within you shifts—how you see, think, and live—so you emerge changed at a fundamental level.

That is my sincere wish for you.

Why This Book Exists

After more than fifteen years of working with leaders, communities, families, and organizations—and through years of doctoral research focused specifically on transformation—I began to see a consistent pattern. People do not struggle because they lack strategies. They struggle because they lack connection: connection to themselves, to others, and to their own story.

I first saw this in peacebuilding projects, working across communities navigating high-stakes conflict. I saw it while working for a global training and consulting firm, helping leaders implement strategy and drive results. And eventually, I saw it most clearly when I helped build a philanthropic leadership institute called **Groundwork**—the primary arc line of this book.

Groundwork was born out of philanthropy. A donor believed our community deserved more than surface-level collaboration and incremental change. The vision was simple but audacious: bring leaders from across sectors—business, nonprofit, government, education, healthcare—into a year-long cohort designed not merely to network, but to catalyze transformation in their communities.

The program was rigorous and deeply human. It spanned twelve months. It combined world-class curriculum, research-informed frameworks, immersive retreats, practical application, and honest dialogue. Leaders practiced, not just learned. They wrestled with purpose. They built a common language. They confronted vulnerability. They formed deep and trusting relationships across sectors that rarely intersect meaningfully.

What we witnessed was not behavior modification. It was identity-level transformation.

My own path prepared me for this work in unexpected ways. I earned a bachelor's degree in intercultural peacebuilding, a master's degree from Creighton University's law school in negotiation and conflict resolution, and eventually a PhD in industrial and organizational psychology. My professional life—including time serving as a healthcare executive—has been oriented toward understanding people.

Along the way, I was shaped by longstanding traditions in conflict transformation, relational leadership, and dialogic practice. Thinkers such as Victor Frankl, Soren Kierkegaard, John Paul Lederach, the Arbinger Institute, Carl Jung, Martin Buber, Terry Warner, and others helped form the soil in which my thinking developed.

The 7 Conditions did not emerge in isolation from that broader conversation, but through doctoral research, sustained qualitative inquiry, and years of lived application within specific communities. What follows is not a claim of invention detached from lineage, but a synthesis refined through practice, culture, and experience.

Across life and leadership.
Across homes and organizations.
Across the communities we inhabit.

And across every context—from corporate boardrooms to school districts to families trying to heal—the same truth emerged: transformation does not begin with metrics or performance. It begins when people re-root themselves in identity, purpose, culture, and relationship.

Over time, I found more truth, power, and clarity in Indigenous worldviews than in much of contemporary leadership literature—not because modern research lacks value, but because our ancestors understood transformation long before we attempted to quantify it. Modern psychology confirms much of what Indigenous wisdom has always practiced.

This book is where those worlds meet.

I wrote it so you can pause, reflect, and reconnect with the parts of your story that shaped you—and the parts still waiting to emerge.

An Indigenous Welcoming

In the Pacific, where my father is from, there is a belief that has shaped generations: *mana*—the spiritual energy that exists in all living things. Mana infuses the land, the sea, the sky, and every person. It is power. It is connection. It is the reminder that nothing living stands alone.

In many Indigenous Filipino traditions, the head is the most sacred part of the body because it holds the greatest concentration of mana. Long before colonization, elders were honored through a gesture of reverence: a younger person gently pressed the back of an elder's hand to their own forehead, receiving their blessing, wisdom, and power. Growing up in a half-Filipino household, this practice was common for us.

Mano Po –
Filipino greeting,
"Your hand please"
(pictured)

When the Spanish arrived, the language changed, but the heart of the practice endured. The word *mano*—hand—became part of the greeting **Mano Po**, meaning "your hand, please," a request for blessing.

The name shifted.
The culture was pressured.
But the spirit survived.

It survived colonization.
It survived forced religion.
It survived the attempted erasure of Indigenous identity.

Because it was never a transaction. It was a connection.

Transaction, as you will discover in this book, is shallow, forgettable, quick, and often meaningless—much like a handshake.

In that same spirit, I offer you my own *Mano Po*.

A gesture of humility and welcome as you begin this book. A gesture of transformation that, unlike transaction, has depth, meaning, and endurance.

A blessing for the journey you are stepping into.

Where the Seven Conditions Came From

Throughout this book, I hope you discover what took me years to learn: ***transformation is caught, not taught.*** It cannot be forced, predicted, or delivered like a formula. It can only be invited through environment, gesture, habit, rhythm, and process.

These invitations are what I call *conditions*—conditions that, when created in a life, family, organization, or community, reliably lead to transformation. The outcome may look different for everyone, but the conditions themselves remain practical and consistent across contexts.

The 7 Conditions explored in this book—**Purpose, Commitment, Common Language, Vulnerability, Consistency, Deep and Trusting Relationships**, and **Safe Space**—did not appear magically. They emerged through years of research and practice, including:

- Semi-structured interviews
- Observations
- Focus groups
- Participatory research
- Field testing
- Work with leaders, families, youth, executives, organizations, and communities

This work began as academic research.
But it became something much larger.

I am not writing to impress scholars. I am writing to empower human beings. Rather than academic language, I share these findings through story, metaphor, culture, and lived experience—because story teaches what science cannot, and science confirms what story has always known.

Together, they are powerful.

Before You Read Further

Reflection is a superpower most of us rarely use.

Before continuing to Chapter One, take a few minutes to consider the following:

1. How would I describe myself—the good and the bad?

2. What experiences, positive or painful, shaped who I am today?

3. What influences me most right now—faith, fear, work, culture, relationships?

4. What am I most afraid of, and why?

5. What do I believe my potential is—in work, relationships, and impact?

6. What barriers stand between me and that potential?

Then:

- List everything currently causing stress or anxiety.
- Cross out what you cannot control.
- Circle what you can.

The circled items will serve as your compass as you move through this book.

A Promise

I will not claim this book contains everything there is to know about transformation. The field is vast and still emerging. But I will tell you this:

I have witnessed these principles transform leaders, parents, organizations, communities, young people, and entire systems.

I have lived them.
I have taught them.
I have researched them.
I have experienced them.

If you engage with these pages—write in the margins, wrestle with the ideas, sit with them—this book will do something within you. Not because I am the author, but because transformation already lives within you.

The journey ahead is the journey of becoming.

Read patiently. Take your time. Do not rush—transformation cannot be hurried. Use the prompts at the end of each chapter. Reflect. Become.

Know that I am right here with you—not physically, but in sincerity, intention, and connection.

Mano Po.
Let's begin.

Chapter *One*:
"THE HANDSHAKE"

When was the last time you shook somebody's hand? Can you remember it—and did it carry any significance, or was it simply a greeting?

If you're like most people, you probably don't remember the last time you shook someone's hand unless prompted. And even then, it likely didn't carry much meaning. This isn't to say the handshake is unimportant in certain cultures, especially Western culture—it certainly is. Sometimes the handshake commemorates important moments, like getting a diploma, getting a job, or most commonly, the beginning and end of a business transaction.

But that's just it—it's a **transaction.**

In 2020, the global pandemic revealed just how shallow and habitual the handshake had become. It disappeared almost overnight—and yet society carried on. Many people still haven't returned to it. If an entire cultural gesture can be temporarily erased and be barely missed, what does that say about how deeply we were engaging with it?

The handshake is not the enemy. But it has become a symbol of something deeper—the transactional nature of many of our interactions and relationships, both professionally and personally.

The Space Between Us: Vā, Kapwa, and Buber

In Samoa, there is a term called **Vā** (*Vah*). Vā is difficult to translate directly into English, but it broadly means the "space between" us—not physical space, but relational space. Vā can be healthy or toxic, nurturing or harmful. What is profound is that Samoans believe the Vā always exists. You don't choose to "enter" a relationship; you are *always* in relationship.

Vā – (Vah)
Samoan
"Space between us"

Whether you acknowledge it or not, you are connected—to family, friends, colleagues, and even strangers.

Vā is the essence of who we are in relation to others and foundational to Samoans' culture and belief systems. It's truly a beautiful and Indigenous ideology we can glean from in powerful ways today, no matter our culture or background.

In the Philippines, the concept of **Kapwa** (*Kahp-wah*), carries a similar weight. It means:

I am who I am in relation to.

Kapwa –
(Kahp-wah)
Filipino,"I am who
I am in relation to."

Kapwa is the idea that our lives, identities, and humanity are interconnected, meaning, we are in essence "one" with others. While we are certainly individuals, we are not alone in our ideological beliefs. For my ancestors, and even many modern Filipinos, this is literal.

There is no I without you, and no you without I.

There exists a "Kapwa culture" today in the Philippines that moves beyond the you-and-me and into a sort of "us-ness." We are a collective in every essence of the word. There is no neutral Kapwa—only healthy or unhealthy, connected or disconnected. But the connection itself never disappears. This can cause us to think that if we are transactional with others, we are transactional even in our idea of the self—perhaps not taking the time to understand our own mind and spirit deeply.

I cannot understand others unless I understand myself, and vice versa.

A significant focus of this book is to help us understand that connecting with others is equal to better connecting with ourselves.

Philosopher Martin Buber expressed this same truth in different language through **I-It** and **I-Thou**—describing the ways we encounter others. In both ways of being, we are the I—the self and the other—an It or Thou. Either we see them as objects (It) or as beings with full humanity (Thou). I often argue the most important part of his framework is the **hyphen**. That hyphen is the connection—the Vā—the space between us that cannot be removed.

We are always connected to others.

Either:

- **connected in a disconnected way** or
- **connected in a connected way**

And the difference between those two states shapes everything: how we lead, how we parent, how we love, how we work, how we build community.

This is why I bring it up now—because the way we greet people is often the clearest indicator of how we see them. *Intention comes first.* Our way of being precedes behavior. Our approach to the "space between" is already present before a single word is spoken.

A Personal Example: When I Was "Shaking Hands" with My Daughter

To illustrate how regularly transaction shows up in our lives, let me share a moment from early parenthood—one that changed me in ways I could not have anticipated.

When my oldest daughter, Eva, was almost two, my wife and I were deep in the struggle of establishing a bedtime routine for her. She loved most of it—bath time, lotion, pajamas, brushing her hair and teeth (or, more accurately, her sucking the toothpaste off the brush). She enjoyed the process. She enjoyed our presence. She enjoyed the rhythm of it all.

What she didn't enjoy was going to sleep and letting us leave the room. Therefore, the entire process became unenjoyable for me.

She wanted us to stay until she fully drifted off—which often took an hour or more. I'm sure many parents can relate. At the time, I was working full-time, starting my master's degree, and my wife was pregnant with our son. Bedtime, though I hated to admit it, had become an inconvenience for me. A burden. Something I needed to "get through" so I could finally start my evening.

I tried everything.

I watched videos.
Read books.
Asked experienced parents.
Implemented every strategy with the most creative problem-solving I could muster.

Nothing worked.

After two exhausting weeks of making what I thought were creative efforts, I found myself frustrated, sitting in the dark beside her crib once again and thinking of all the other things I'd rather be doing: my homework, catching up on emails, spending time with my wife, or even just binging a show on Netflix. Instead, there I was, waiting for her to fall asleep so I could escape.

One night, she was splashing in the bathtub while I sat on a little stool trying to catch up on school reading. She kept soaking my book. My irritation climbed. But when I turned toward her—ready to correct her—I saw her laughing, smiling, wanting me to play. So, I put the book down and played with my daughter. We had a great time, as always—the efforts leading up to her actually going to sleep were not the problem.

After bath time, as I stood behind her brushing her long, dark hair while she giggled in the mirror, something softened in me. Looking back, the metaphorical handshake began to reveal its transactional nature.

I knew that in just a few minutes, we'd be in the dark room again. And I knew that frustration was waiting for me there. But in that moment—watching my little girl with wet hair, toothpaste on her chin, and joy on her face—I felt a question rise inside me:

Why does this feel so hard?
Why do I dread what should be a sacred moment?
Why am I so transactional with my own child?

A question surfaced that I had always dismissed because I figured she was "too young" to answer clearly. But I asked it anyway.

"Eva... what do you need from Daddy so you can go night-night?"

She turned instantly toward me with her big hazel eyes wide open, holding two little fingers up, and said:

"Daddy, I want you to read two books... and pat me two minutes."

That was it.

So that night, we tried it.

We said goodnight to Mommy.
I intentionally picked the shortest books on her shelf.
We read them—silly voices and laughter between us.
Then she said, "Okay, Daddy, now pat me."

She turned over, showing me her little back.
I gently patted her for maybe ninety seconds, the way parents often do to calm their little ones.
She squinted her eyes shut—signaling she was ready. I couldn't believe it.

"I'm going now," I whispered.
She turned, gave me a big toddler kiss, and I backed out of the room like I was disarming a bomb.

Nothing happened.
No crying.
No screaming.
No meltdown.

This had never happened before.

I checked on her twice that night—once she was awake, whispering to herself, and later, she was asleep.

I sat in my office afterward, stunned. How could all my attempts to fix this problem fail, just to have the answer be this simple?

And that's when the truth hit me: **I had been seeing and treating my daughter transactionally—like a task, a routine, a box to check. A problem to fix, instead of a relationship to connect with. A handshake.**

I was ignoring her humanity.
I was neglecting the Vā between us.
I was living the opposite of Kapwa.
And I hadn't even seen it. But, I realized, she felt it all along.

That night changed me. Eva was not responding to my "tactics" or my surface-level efforts; she was responding to the space between us, the Vā, our relationship.

Our Kapwa began transforming that night.

I saw every bedtime routine as an opportunity to strengthen my relationship with my little one. I began to ask what she needed instead of forcing what was convenient for me. Some nights, it was two books and pats. Other nights, it was "Sing a song," "Tell me a story," or "Daddy, do a silly dance." None of it took long. And they became some of the most cherished moments of my life—so cherished that my wife sometimes had to intervene because we were having too much fun.

To think that I almost missed it all because I was "shaking hands" with my own daughter devastates me.

And if you're like me, you know this isn't just about bedtime routines. This is about life, work, and our communities.
About relationships.
About how often we move through the world transactionally, without even noticing.

(Years later, during another bedtime moment, Eva taught me the opposite of transaction—Unggno, "sharing the breath of life." But that belongs to the next chapter.)

A Millionaire's Question

I hope that brief example with my daughter resonates but let me share how this entire journey of research and understanding transformation began. Because what has unfolded in my life since then has given me more than many may receive in an entire lifetime.

Many years ago, early in my career, I had the opportunity to sit knee-to-knee with a philanthropist—a true self-made man who had accumulated hundreds of millions in wealth. Now in his seventies, he spends nearly all his time giving back to his community. I had met his son and a business partner at a workshop put on by the company I worked for at the time, and after several weeks of building a relationship with them, they wanted me to meet this man.

He flew me up to Salem, Oregon, just to have a conversation about possibilities and life. We talked for almost an hour about what brought us joy, the importance of leadership, family, community, and the work we each cared deeply about. At the end of the conversation, he asked me a question that would alter the course of my life:

"Chris, if you could make a difference in this community—if you could help transform it—and you didn't have to worry about resources, what would you do?"

I must have looked stunned because he quickly added, "Don't answer yet. Take a few days. Think. Pray. Reflect. Then send me your answer. Just a few bullet points."

I took his request seriously. I spent two days thinking, wrestling, writing, revising, and reflecting. Then I sent him a simple plan—no more than a few bullet points.

Within minutes, he replied: **"I like it. Let's get to work."**

That moment set me on a journey that forever changed me. That philanthropist became a dear friend and mentor. The opportunities that followed introduced me to leaders, communities, challenges, and discoveries I could have never predicted. Much of the content of this book traces back to that single question, asked in humility and generosity.

An "OK" Plan That Led to a Critical Awakening

At the top of my plan, I wrote: "Work with leaders throughout the community."

I believed transformational change required leaders to come together—collaborating, building trust, learning, growing. I had no idea whether that was already happening. I had no data. I wasn't from the community of Salem. I didn't know where to start. I was primarily guided by intuition and the little experience I had.

My background was in peacebuilding, conflict resolution, and organizational development. I didn't yet have my PhD. I was nearing the end of my master's program. And although I didn't have much experience, I did have passion. And this philanthropist—technically now my boss—had the resources to help turn possibility into reality. The deal was, in his words, "I'll write the check, and you do the work."

So, I got to work.

For the first three months, I met with a new leader or community member almost every day. I attended more community events than I can even remember. I became ingrained in certain circles of influence. I began planting the seeds of *transformational change* everywhere I went.

Another part of my plan was to facilitate leadership development and community trainings—collaboration, innovation, civic engagement, and more. With the resources at my disposal, I began hosting workshops monthly, then bi-monthly, then quarterly.

After three years, we had trained over **3,000 people**.

It looked impressive.
It felt impressive.
But the truth?

We had almost no evidence of transformational change.

We had some good stories, inspiring moments, and positive feedback—but nothing that demonstrated deep, sustained impact. I started to feel disheartened—if we can't figure this out with endless resources at our backs, then maybe it's just not possible.

That was a painful realization.

Many of us, personally and professionally, throw resources at solving problems in our relationships and cultures, left with only the "efforts" we put in to show for it. We realize that training may give information and create compliance, and resources can help work move along. But none of that ensures transformational change... only transactional. As in the story of my daughter and me, I tried every trick and every piece of parenting advice—but nothing worked. Something was clearly missing; I just didn't know what.

Transactional Leadership: Surface-Minded

I had to confront something uncomfortable during this time: **we are far more transactional as leaders than we want to admit.**

We shake hands with everyone—literally and metaphorically. We act politely. We say the right things. We nod. We smile. We show up.

But internally, many of us are guarded, distracted, disconnected, and surface-minded.

As I shared previously—and it hurts to admit still— I defined my relationship with my daughter before I finally realized I needed to change.

Imagine soil. A surface-minded person only pays attention to what grows above the soil—the plants, fruit, weeds, and leaves—without paying attention to what lies beneath: the roots, nutrients, depth, and soil quality. You can do the right things on the surface, but if the roots are weak or the soil is depleted, nothing truly transforms.

We can "do leadership" in a surface-minded way.
We can "do relationships" in a surface-minded way.
We can "do life" in a surface-minded way.

And we might even be praised for it.
But surface-minded action produces surface-level outcomes.

The Day I Realized I Was the Problem

One afternoon, I attended a major community event filled with the well-known leaders of the city—the "who's who." The purpose was noble: to address pressing issues affecting children, families, and vulnerable populations.

I arrived early, observing hundreds of leaders as they socialized. Music played. People greeted each other with smiles, **handshakes**, and small talk. Laughter filled the room.

As I watched, with this realization of transactional leadership on my mind, I wondered:

"How many of these leaders genuinely mean what they're expressing? How many of these interactions are sincere? And how many are simply... transactions?"

I felt strangely self-righteous in that moment, as if I had discovered a secret truth about everyone else: their transactional leadership styles.

Then I made eye contact with a leader I didn't particularly like. Of course, he had no idea I felt this way. As he approached, I stood up to greet him— as we are trained to do—and without hesitation, with a smile on my face, I extended my hand.

We shook hands. And I heard myself say: **"It's nice to see you."** Except… it wasn't. And I knew it. He probably felt it!

In an instant, I realized I had done the very thing I was silently judging everyone else for. I was performing. Posturing. Going through the motions.

I felt ashamed.

As I sat back down in my seat and as the meeting began, I realized, painfully:

I wasn't just diagnosing the problem. I was contributing to it.

If I wanted to help create transformation, I had to transform myself first— beginning with how I greeted, saw, and related to people.

My realization that leadership in our community is so transactional was certainly true, but I was the guilty one. I was so swept up in the under- standing that I was both VERY right in my realization of the transactional leadership problem, but so VERY wrong in how I pointed blame and judged others. Here I was, preaching transformation and change in meetings, gatherings, training, etc., yet I didn't even see the fraud in myself.

Have you ever had a similar experience ? Maybe you shook someone's hand, engaged in a token nicety, or something of the like, but didn't mean it. It has been my experience since that moment that we as people and especial- ly leaders often create careers out of doing the "right things," but in the "wrong way." We literally and metaphorically "shake hands" with everyone and everything we encounter, engaging in transactions wherever we go.

Why This Matters

We might think, what's the big deal? Why does it matter? Well, a few things: it mattered to me that day; it probably mattered to that gentleman; it matters to you whether the people in your life mean it when they offer you nice gestures. In fact, you can probably recall multiple instances when you felt someone's disdin or inauthentic behavior toward you, even though they apeared acceptable on the surface. If you're brave enough, think of the last time you were the one acting inauthentic or transactional. I would venture that the answers to those questions could be as recent as today or yesterday. This is how common and constant Buber's I-It and I-Thou are at play. This is why the concepts of Kapwa and Vā are so incredible to learn from.

However, the biggest problem with this is that we often long for transformational outcomes; we desire deep or lasting change in many of our relationships, families, businesses, and communities. But we start our interactions off with transactions and surface-deep gestures.

How can we expect transformational outcomes if our foundation and initial greetings begin with a transaction?

Whether literal or metaphorical, there is no denying that our lives are frothed with transactions. Relationships are built and maintained through transactions. Families sometimes operate transactionally with endless checklists and activities. Organizations create processes and procedures to orchestrate and maintain transactions. And our communities do the same through endless policy. It's the definition of insanity: doing the same things (in different ways, perhaps) over and over but expecting different results. Crazy, right?

Here is the uncomfortable truth:

We desire deep, lasting, transformational outcomes—in our families, relationships, leadership, organizational culture, and community.

But we begin our interactions with surface-level transactions.

We plant seeds in shallow soil and wonder why nothing grows.
We "shake hands" with life and expect life to transform us.
It doesn't work that way.

Transformation cannot emerge from a transactional foundation.

Not in leadership. Not in community work.
Not in families. Not in marriages.
Not in faith. Not anywhere.

If the **roots** are transactional, the **fruit** will be transactional.

After this brief exchange of shaking hands with this gentleman, and this profound realization that transformation cannot be possible when conceived out of transaction, I realized my entire approach needed to change. I was not just part of the solution; I was part of the problem. Even more, I needed to change the way I greeted others first, perhaps not literally but certainly metaphorically. How could I greet someone with a gesture other than the typical transactional handshake and begin our interaction with the momentum and even "spirit" of transformation? Was it possible, and would that even make a difference?

With this fresh perspective in mind, I had a realization that would change everything. It started with me intentionally breaking free from the internal expectation of a transactional handshake and embracing something different, something deeper, something transformational—a simple gesture and greeting near and dear to me: the breath of life.

But that is what the next chapter is about. Right now, I want you to reflect upon a couple of questions. As I asked in the preface, take out something to write with. Remember, reflection is a superpower, and I will consistently ask you to reflect on critical questions I promise will contribute to your transformation as you read this book.

Reflection

Before moving to the next chapter, take a moment to reflect. Write your answers down. Don't skip this.

What are you doing right now in your life that is surface-deep and transactional? It might be a literal handshake—or something more personal.

____

____

____

____

____

What percentage of your day do you feel you are simply "going through the motions?" Why is that harmful to your ability to reach your potential?

____

____

____

____

____

Transformation begins not when we change other people, but when we change the way we relate—starting with the simplest of gestures.

Chapter *Two:*
THE BREATH OF LIFE

Not learning and then benefiting from Indigenous and ancestral cultures is robbing us of timeless wisdom.

In the preface of this book, I referenced that an important part of my heritage is being from the Philippines. In the Philippines, and across the greater Asia-Pacific islands, there exists a greeting dating back long before colonialism—an Indigenous gesture of my ancestors.

*Unggno –
(Uhn-go)*
Ilocano

It goes by many names, and while language and customs have shifted across generations and colonization, the gesture and its meaning remain the same. In the Philippines, where my father is from, this greeting can be called **Unggno** (*Uhn-go*). In New Zealand, my Māori brothers and sisters call it **Hongi** (*Hong-ee*). In Hawaii, it is **Honi** (*Ho-nee*). In Samoa, it is called **Feasogi** (*Feh-ah-soh-gee*).

*Hongi –
(Hong-ee)*
Māori

*Honi –
(Ho-nee)*
Hawaiian

The gesture is simple, intentional, and profoundly human: two people gently press their foreheads and noses together, close their eyes, and take a deep, intentional breath.

*Feasongi –
(Feh-ah-soh-gee)*
Samoan

It ultimately means to **share "the breath of life."**

It is beautiful. It is grounding.
It is sacred. It is real.

For those unfamiliar with these Indigenous practices, this gesture might feel uncomfortable, vulnerable, or even intrusive. But to me, to my fellow islanders, and to my ancestors, the Unggno is a gesture of respect, intention, and human recognition. Even with strangers, it signals:

I see you. Your humanity matters.
We share something sacred.

It is a greeting filled with meaning and purpose. It honors the Vā—the space between us—and the Kapwa—the "I am who I am in relation to." It is the opposite of transactional in every way. It is I–Thou made physical. It is the beginning of transformational relationships.

If I can take you back to the moment from the previous chapter, as I was sitting in that community meeting after my own transactional handshake, this gesture—the Unggno—came flooding into my mind. The opposite of the handshake. The antidote. The counterpart.

I imagined greeting that gentleman not with a closed-off handshake, but with the Unggno. And instantly, everything inside me shifted. Just picturing it softened my heart. I could see his humanity. It made the judgment in me quiet down and the compassion rise up.

It made me ask:

What if leaders greeted each other this way?
What if we began our interactions from intention, not performance?
What if transformation started with breath?

Weeks passed with these thoughts bouncing around my mind, but before I share how that came to life, I need to tell you a story—one that changed me in a way no research, workshop, or leadership training ever could.

It came, again, from my daughter, Eva, during another bedtime moment.

The Breath of Life, Taught by a Four-Year-Old

The moment from the previous chapter—that painful realization I had been "shaking hands" with my own daughter while treating her bedtime needs as a transaction—changed me. It opened my eyes to the Vā between us and allowed us to form some of the most cherished memories of my early fatherhood.

But a couple of years later, she taught me something even deeper.

Eva was then around four years old. Bedtime had become easy for her. She was proud of going to bed like a "big girl." I was still in graduate school and close to finishing while also working full-time and doing intense work with this philanthropist. Most nights, the moment the kids went down, my workday picked back up. My wife, now a mother of two little ones, would often graciously tell me, despite her own exhaustion, "Go get your work done. I'll handle bedtime tonight."

But one evening, Eva had other plans.

Out of nowhere, she regressed as if she were two years old again—crying, resisting, clinging, refusing to settle. My wife started out patient, but frustration escalated quickly. I could hear the tension from down the hall.

Something in me snapped into protective husband mode.
I wasn't calm. I was firm. Too firm.

I walked into Eva's room with seriousness on my face, bent down, and, without hurting her, clasped her cheeks firmly in my hands. I looked straight at her and said:

"You better go to sleep right now and stop disrespecting your mother!"

Her crying stopped mid-breath. Tears kept falling. Her eyes widened with fear. And she turned away from me, curling toward the wall like she wanted to disappear.

I knew instantly that I had gone too far. Shame swept through me.

I walked out and sat on the couch as guilt settled over me. Yes, she needed to listen. Yes, she needed to respect her mother. But my tone... my approach... my intensity... and the look of fear on her face...

I failed her in that moment.

Seeing my guilt, my wife tried to comfort me: "It's okay. She'll be fine tomorrow. Don't beat yourself up."

But I couldn't shake it. I couldn't work.
I couldn't concentrate. I couldn't rest.

An hour later, I did what my guilt was begging me to do. I went to her room to apologize.

I cracked open the door. The hallway light cut across the darkness. She looked asleep, still facing the wall.

Still, I quietly went in.

I knelt by her bed and with tears welling up in my eyes, I whispered:

"Angel... I'm so sorry. I want to be a good daddy. A better daddy. You didn't deserve that. I shouldn't have gotten mad. I love you so much."

I spoke barely above a whisper, not wanting to wake her but needing to say it out loud, like a prayer or confession.

Then she moved, awake the entire time.

She slowly turned toward me. She sat up, sleepy-eyed, still warm from rest. She reached her little hands out...

... and gently held my face.
Then she leaned forward and pressed her forehead to mine.
Unggno. The breath of life.

A four-year-old child, without prompting or explanation, instinctively shared the gesture of my ancestors with me.

And then she whispered: **"You're a good daddy. I love you. You can go to bed."**

In that moment, everything in me broke open. The guilt loosened.
The connection was restored. The space between us healed.

Where only an hour before I had held her face and looked into her eyes with frustration, she was now holding my face and looking into my eyes with love. She showed me that transformation is breath-to-breath.

Humanity-to-humanity. Presence-to-presence. Grace-to-grace.

I will never forget that night. Eva taught me the heart of Unggno. Not academically. Not theoretically. But spiritually.

She shared the breath of life with me when I needed it most. Consider how many people in your life, at home and work, need you to share the breath of life with them, What would improve? How would things get better by first, simply considering moving beyond the nature of a "handshake?"

I have learned that people in our lives are longing for connection. They may not need you to literally Unggno with them but they want to be seen and recognized. And for both your sake and theirs, the space between you and them has an unseen potential to improve.

A Return to the Moment From Chapter One

Thinking back to the community meeting where I shook hands with the gentleman I didn't like, I imagined greeting him through Unggno. The opposite of the handshake. The antidote to transaction. And instantly, everything changed.

If I had greeted him that way—even metaphorically—I would have seen him differently, cared for him differently, and entered the interaction with more humanity. The words, "it's nice to see you," might have meant something.

That realization stayed with me for weeks as I wondered how to translate this discovery into the work we were doing in the community with leaders and their organizations.

Then I finally had the chance to bring it to life.

The Leadership Institute:
A Deeply-Minded Approach

One of our major community efforts was the creation of a twelve-month leadership institute, Groundwork. Each year, we would select fifteen to thirty influential leaders from all sectors of the community and bring them through a year-long journey of learning, relationship-building, and deep reflection. The journey began with a three-day retreat on the Oregon coast.

We wanted the retreat to feel different—set apart from anything they had experienced before.

I knew this was my chance. Not to ask them to perform the literal gesture, but to invite them into its meaning—intention, vulnerability, humanity, connection.

On the final day, I approached a colleague who had helped me design this institute, a respected leader named Salam (whom I will talk about more in a later chapter, as he was a critical piece in this journey) and asked if he would help me demonstrate the Unggno to the group. I explained the gesture, its meaning, and its purpose. I asked for his consent, knowing it was vulnerable.

To my gratitude, he said "yes."

We returned to the group. I explained the history, the significance, and the essence of the gesture. Then Salam and I placed our hands on each other's shoulders, gently pressed our foreheads and noses together, closed our eyes, and took a deep, intentional breath.

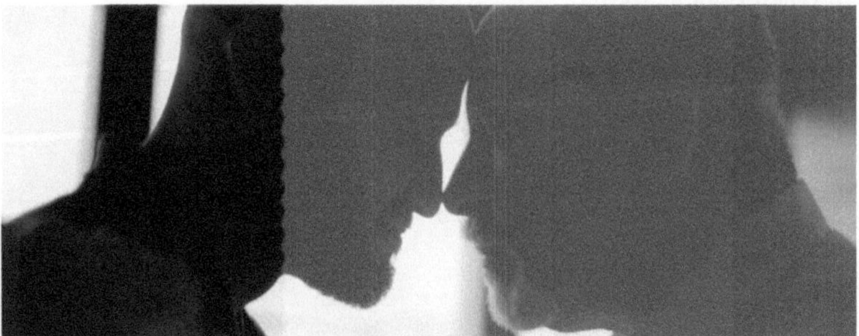

It was powerful.
Sacred and still.
Deep and transformational.

I have performed the Unggno many times with family and close friends, but this time was different. This time, it was the gateway to something bigger.

When we opened our eyes, Salam—typically stoic, reserved, composed—was visibly moved. Tears filled his eyes as he shared with the group what it meant to him.

He felt connected to me.
He felt responsible for me.
He felt something shift inside.
He felt the humanity of the moment.

There was not a dry eye amongst us. Then, in near silence, another leader raised their hand. "Can we... do this with each other?" I didn't hesitate: "Absolutely."

One by one, leaders stood up.
One by one, they pressed foreheads and noses together.
One by one, they shared breath.
One by one, they caught transformation.

It was unlike anything I had ever seen.
It was so much different than that handshake.

For a few moments, every leader in that room tapped into something ancient, human, and deeply transformative—this deeper mindset and understanding of relationship. We *caught* transformation. For years, I had been trying to *teach* transformation, over and over. Yet this day, I realized something incredibly profound.

Transformation is caught, not taught.

To this day, it remains one of the most meaningful moments of my entire career.

Every cohort from that point forward began with the Unggno—sometimes literally, always metaphorically.

And the outcomes? Too many to list, but here are some highlights.

- Marriages restored
- People healing from depression and anxiety
- Leaders finding confidence they had lost
- Organizational cultures shifting
- Organizations transforming
- Communities collaborating in ways we never imagined
- Problems once thought impossible suddenly becoming solvable

All from an ancient gesture that begins with breath.

Transformation Is Caught, Not Taught

Despite all the hours I've spent studying transformation, all the coaching, all the facilitating, all the leadership development, I have yet to find anything as powerful as the Unggno for helping people **catch** transformation.

Because that is the secret: *transformation is caught, not taught.*

My job in this book is not to convince or lecture you into transformation. It is to help you catch it—through reflection, story, breath, meaning, and intention. I know your lives, organizations, and communities are frothed with transaction. Some of you may not want to admit it, or maybe you still don't see it as a problem. But keep reading and you will see the potential of what can become in the pages of this book.

And that begins right now.

An Unggno Exercise

Think of someone in your life who is in need of transformation—a relationship that needs healing, deepening, or reconnecting.

Picture this person clearly.
Their eyes.
Their face.
Their expressions.
Their presence.

Close your eyes and imagine pressing your forehead and nose to theirs, gently, intentionally.
Imagine taking a deep breath together.
Go.

...

Open your eyes.

What did you feel?
What changed?
What softened?

What would shift if you greeted them—literally or metaphorically—in this way the next time you saw them?

Try it. Truly.

The breath of life changes the Vā between us.
And it changes us.

Your Invitation

No reflection questions in this chapter—only an invitation: go and share the breath of life.

Literally, if the relationship and circumstances permit, do so respectfully to my culture and that of my ancestors. But most certainly do so metaphorically. No matter how you greet them—a handshake, an embrace, or even a nod of recognition, do so with the deep intent of sharing the breath of life.

While nothing can replace the power of the literal gesture, I am not ignorant of others sense of boundaries and cultural customs. But my hope is that by now, you understand the meaning and intent behind the Unggno and the sharing of the breath of life.

It will catalyze transformation in your relationships.

With those you love.
With those you lead.
With those you serve.
With those you struggle with.

Greet them differently.
See them differently.
Start differently.

Begin with breath. Begin with transformation.
Because once you do, you will begin to catch it in your life.

Chapter *Three*:
"WE HAD TO PUSH RECORD"

At first, the breath of life felt like a spark—unexpected, clarifying, holy. But sparks, if they matter, become flame. And flame, if tended, becomes a steady heat you can live by. That's what happened across our leadership institute. What began as a startling moment of presence—Unggno—matured into a quiet, steady pulse that leaders carried into the ordinary: meetings, classrooms, job sites, council chambers, and kitchen tables. They didn't just reference the breath of life; they **practiced** it—awkward at first, then honest, then natural. Slowly, what used to be modules, agendas, and protocols took on weight. Everything we had built suddenly felt **alive**.

At the time, none of us were walking around saying, "This is the thing." We weren't sure *what* to call it. It didn't ask for attention. It certainly didn't demand it. But it anchored our team and the leaders we were working with. Quietly, it turned the keys to doors we'd been rattling for years.

We were in the middle of it—moment by moment, room by room—so much so that we could **feel** it before we could name it. "It" being the seedlings of transformation. There's a point in any genuine work where you realize the story is moving faster than your language. That's where we were.

So, we did the one thing we knew we had to do.

We pushed record.

We started capturing what was happening because it was too important and too fragile to trust to memory alone. We wrote it down. We documented conversations. We paid attention to patterns. We listened for the through line beneath the noise.

As we did, the fog started to lift. Conversations started to have a rhythm, patterns began to emerge, and the realization that we were discovering something truly transformational was becoming a reality.

Relationships that had been purely transactional began to deepen. Leaders who used to update and report began to reveal and reflect. Vulnerability showed up not as a performance, but as a presence. The surface-level exchanges gave way to something riskier and more real. I witnessed rooms shift because one person told the truth—and then another did, and then another. That's the rhythm of transformation: one voice makes it possible, a second makes it safe, and then the room takes a breath together.

We saw the outcomes in lives, not just in notes.

A business owner and longtime nonprofit board member on the brink of divorce found his marriage not only salvaged but **renewed**. He credited the institute for the change, not because we taught marriage content (we didn't), but because something in him shifted. Presence softened shame. Language gave form to what he was feeling. Courage moved the conversation from "what's wrong" to "what's possible." Nearly a year after beginning his journey in our institute, his words about his marriage were, "It's better than it's ever been."

Another leader entered our work under the weight of diagnosed anxiety and depression. They were already under professional care long before our institute. And yet, months into the journey, they described a profound difference in their mental health—the kind you don't fake. No change in job. No move. No windfall. Just one new variable: deep, repeated engagement in this work—showing up to honest spaces, naming truth, practicing connection, and building rituals of meaning. They felt different **from the inside out.**

We didn't design a course to save marriages. We didn't run a curriculum for mental health. Yet those were some of the clearest fruits. The outcomes were never the "point," but they kept showing up—evidence that transformation doesn't compartmentalize. When people catch it, it spills everywhere into their lives.

Confidence rose. Some leaders shifted roles to align with meaning, not just momentum. Others stayed where they were but led differently—less performative, more real, more human. A few were promoted and used their new seats to do what they'd learned with us: drive purpose, be vulnerable, and create sacred space where people could tell the truth and still belong. Other leaders who had enough lived experience to write a shelf of books finally started **claiming** their voices. The decisions got better. The rooms got lighter. The work got deeper.

And then something we could measure started happening too.

Bottom lines improved. Partnerships formed across corners of the city that hadn't spoken in years. Stuck dialogues moved. New approaches—practical, not trendy—rose out of the conversations. You can call that innovation if you like, but it felt more like integrity—people doing the next right thing, again and again.

The patterns were too consistent to ignore, and it would have been dishonest not to ask *why*. We needed to be intentional in capturing what was happening.

So, we moved from noticing to **knowing**. From "this is happening" to "what's actually at work here?" We pushed record by the intentionality of evaluation and research. Frankly, we literally pressed record as we gathered video case-studies, sharing some of these remarkable stories of transformation.

We built a research frame—structured enough to be credible, flexible enough to be human. We moved beyond anecdotes without despising them. We honored story while adding rigor. We gathered data through direct observation, semi-structured interviews, focus groups, and participatory research. We coded themes. We tracked moments. We mapped what we were seeing against what people were actually doing, saying, and feeling.

We brought in an independent third party each year to evaluate the institute—what needed to change, what clearly worked, and what deserved a second life. We committed to academic integrity without losing the soul of the work. That balance was non-negotiable: *methods in service to meaning.* We would not allow the purpose-driven work to become subject to discovery and research. The meaning and purpose always came before our methods of discovery.

We set out to create transformation in our community, and that would remain the top priority.

It wasn't clean. It never is. Trust had to be earned—sometimes leader by leader, sometimes organization by organization. In some rooms, the past walked in before the people did—old wounds, old stories, old scores. We learned to listen differently. We learned to sit longer. We learned to begin meetings with presence and not rush to "content." We learned to let quiet do some of the work. We learned not to confuse volume with impact.

And then the shape began to appear.

First as a silhouette, then as a sketch, and eventually as a living framework we could test and strengthen.

We didn't set out to discover "seven" of anything. There was no clever number waiting for us on a whiteboard. We weren't hunting for a tidy model. We were hunting for truth. But over time—month after month, year after year—the signal separated from the noise. What arose were seven interlocking conditions that, when present and practiced in sequence, turned sparks into sustainable heat.

Purpose. Commitment. Common Language. Vulnerability. Consistency. Deep and Trusting Relationships. Safe Space to Learn and Practice.

We began to organize our institute around them, not as content to deliver but as **conditions** to steward. The order mattered. The repetition mattered. The way we held the room mattered. So did how we ended the day and how we began the next one. Small things weren't small.

But alongside those seven, something else—older than our research and deeper than our programming—kept surfacing.

It was there before we could name it.
It infused the room whenever presence replaced performance.
It turned strangers into neighbors and adversaries into partners.
It was my inheritance speaking to my practice.
It was the ancient meeting the modern.

Later, we would name it **Culture of One**.

If the 7 Conditions were discovered through research, Culture of One was **revealed** through remembrance. I did not invent it. I recognized it. It was the through line I had been living without language the entire time: my Indigenous practices and beliefs; the breath of life; the wisdom of **Pamana** (*pah-mah-NAH*); the shared identity of Kapwa; the sacred present of Un-ggno. Those weren't "inspirations." They were the **catalyst**—the way the room became capable of transformation at all. I cannot overstate that the 7 Conditions came *after* we figured out a way to catalyze transformation, and that catalyst was what I now call Culture of One: *the meeting of past, present, and future.* This is the key connection and distinction between the 7 Conditions and Culture of One. I want this to be crystal clear as we continue through this book, because everything hinges on them.

> Pamana–
> (pah-mah-NAH)
> Filipino,
> "Inheritance, legacy/
> lineage, or heritage"

I can admit this now: I don't know if I would have seen it without the work. And I don't know if the work would have held without it.

Here's what I also learned in the years since: the Indigenous awakening that shaped Culture of One does not have to be *mine* for you to live it. Your lineage, your stories, your rituals, your culture, and your community carry their own wisdom. The point isn't to borrow my practices. The point is to **remember** and realize yours. Culture of One is not about technique; it's about truth. It's not about trends; it's about **roots.**

And the 7 Conditions? They aren't novel as words. You've heard them. You've probably taught some of them. The difference is how they **live** together, in order, over time, and in rooms and organizations that are tended with care. Their power isn't in their vocabulary. It's in their **sequence, repetition, and stewardship,** all threaded together by *intentionality.*

Since those first cohorts, I've tested and retested these conditions in consulting, in organizational assessments, and in my own leadership as a healthcare executive. Each time, the lesson deepens: the conditions are invitational, not mechanical; lived, not laminated; human, not just organizational.

In the chapters ahead, I will open each one. Not as a theory, but as a practice you can hold in your hands. We'll explore how Purpose reclaims meaning from Pamana. How Commitment chooses and keeps choosing. How Common Language helps us remember who we are. How Vulnerability opens the door that fear guards. How Consistency does ordinary things with sacred intention. How Deep and Trusting Relationships make bonds unbreakable. How Safe Space to Learn and Practice turns failure and blemish into courage and becoming.

Here's how I frame them for a more personal approach for you and your families/teams to resonate with.

1. **Purpose** = You Came From Something, Now Become Something

2. **Commitment** = Choose—and Then Keep Choosing

3. **Common Language** = Discover Words That Remind You Who You Are in the Good Times and the Bad

4. **Vulnerability** = Open the Door That Fear Tells You to Keep Shut

5. **Consistency** = Do Ordinary Things With Sacred Intention

6. **Trusting Relationships** = Go Deep, Not Wide—Build Something That Withstands the Storms

7. **Safe Space** = Create Space for Becoming

We didn't just push record back then. I'm **still** pushing record. I am still a student of transformation, not its master. The work keeps teaching me and I intend to let it until my last day. I suspect I'll still be mesmerized by its simple complexity when I'm old and gray.

Here is my invitation to you as you turn the page and step into Culture of One and the Conditions themselves:

Push record in your own life.

Write down what you feel. Note what you notice. Capture the small wins and the honest misses. Pay attention to the room when presence replaces performance. Pay attention to your body when you tell the truth and the room doesn't shatter. Pay attention to the lift you feel when you choose connection over control.

Those aren't side notes.
They're the evidence.
They're the transformation.
They're the beginning of your own research.

Because what we learned by recording is what you will discover by living:

Transformation is not a moment you manufacture. It is a movement you recognize, a truth you remember, and a practice you **repeat**—together.

Push record.

Reflection

How are you currently pushing record in your own life i.e., a journal, etc.?

____

____

____

____

Is your family intentional in understanding their history, and documenting it real time?

____

____

____

____

Is your organization intentional in documenting through video, blog, newsletters, etc?

____

____

____

____

If the answer is no to any of the above, find a way to start now.

Chapter *Four*:
CULTURE OF ONE

Remember, breathe, become.

Transformation is possible.
Not someday, not when life slows down, not when you finally feel ready.

Right now.

You have what you need for transformation within you, around you, and between you and others. This book is not here to give you something new. It is here to help you recognize what has been there all along.

Yet we live in a world where the word *transformation* has lost its weight. It is used constantly and understood rarely.

Organizations put it in mission statements.
Leaders declare it as a strategy.
Companies invest in programs built around it.

The word is everywhere. But the meaning is disappearing.

Transformation has become a buzzword—a disguised substitute for what most people are actually aiming for: **change**.

Whether we admit it or not, most people don't pursue transformation. They pursue **change** but change and transformation are not the same.

Change is external. It is behavioral. It can be engineered, purchased, or managed.

- You can follow a program and change.
- You can hire consultants and change.
- You can update systems and change.
- You can comply and change.

Change is something you do.
Transformation is something you become.

Change happens at the surface.
Transformation happens at the root.

Change can impress others.
Transformation reshapes the self.

People can comply their way into change—
but they can never comply their way into transformation.

Transformation is internal.
It reshapes how you see, think, and behave from the inside out.

Change touches behavior.
Transformation touches identity.

Change can be forced.
Transformation must be chosen.

Change may appear different.
Transformation **feels** different.

This is why so many organizations believe they have transformed when all they have actually done is reorganized. They measure surface-level outcomes and call it transformation. But nothing is different beneath the surface. The relationships don't change. The culture doesn't change. The space between people doesn't change.

Transformation is not what happens on a spreadsheet. Transformation is what happens in the unseen space between human beings.

Which brings us to Culture of One, the catalyst to discovering the 7 Conditions.

The Moment Everything Changed

Culture of One did not come to me in a meeting or a whiteboard session. It did not arrive through a leadership model or a book.

It came in the most ordinary moment—when I simply imagined greeting someone I did not like using *Unggno*, the breath of life, a gesture from my Filipino heritage.

It was instinctive. Quick. Unplanned. A tiny act of humanity.
But afterward, something struck me.

For years, I had been building leadership programs about connection, empathy, and community... but I had not been embodying them.

I had been present physically and intellectually—but absent spiritually and emotionally.

That interaction was transactional up until the second I breathed life into it.

In that moment, an ancient cultural memory met a modern leadership problem. And the solution was not technical,it was human.

Transformation wasn't something we needed to create. It was something we needed to **remember** and **discover** within ourselves.

Culture of One was born not from theory, but from rediscovery. It revealed a truth that changed the entire trajectory of my work:

We already have what we need to catalyze transformation. We simply forget where to look.

And once I understood that, everything shifted.

Meetings became different. Conflict softened.
Leaders who were previously guarded began opening up.

The room itself felt different—less mechanical, more human.

Suddenly, transformation did not require more money, more programs, or more expertise. It required **presence, remembrance, and connection.**

The work became lighter—not easier, but more alive.

This is why Culture of One matters:

- It removes the lie that you are behind.
- It removes the lie that transformation is far away.
- It removes the lie that someone else has the answers.

This discovery laid the foundation for what would become the 7 Conditions of Transformation. These conditions were not invented in a vacuum. They were learned by watching transformation breathe in real rooms, among real leaders, facing real complexity.

Culture of One is the philosophy. The 7 Conditions are the practice.

One awakens the possibility. The other sustains the reality.

But before we get there, we must begin where transformation always begins:

With the past.

PAMANA—THE PAST

Pamana means inheritance or legacy. It is the understanding that the past is not behind us, it is beneath us. It is the soil holding up everything we are trying to grow.

In Western thinking, the past is treated like something to escape:

- "Don't look back."
- "The past doesn't matter."
- "Just move on."

But Indigenous wisdom—and the psychology of healing—say something different.

Trauma research tells us that what remains unintegrated in the past repeats itself in the present. Organizational development research says the same: companies that ignore their origin stories lose identity, culture, and direction. Communities that forget their history repeat their wounds.

The past is not the enemy. The past is the teacher.

When we began building a community-wide leadership initiative, I thought we were creating something new. I believed we were innovating where no path existed.

But Pamana taught me something different:

Nothing meaningful begins from scratch.

Every decision we made was rooted in the sacrifices, failures, and courage of those who came before—philanthropists, founders, educators, organizers, families, traditions, and trial and error.

My friend and donor believed transformation was possible because he had lived through the darkness of watching his community fracture. He had seen loss. He had poured years into rebuilding.

His Pamana—his story—was the invisible root system that carried our entire effort.

The work wasn't new. It was inherited.
Pamana shows up everywhere. Consider the following:

In Families

A child raised by a single mother learns grit because she watched grit lived. We may even learn what *not* to do, based on the failures of parents or grandparents. Their mistakes become our turning points.

In Organizations

A founder's values shape a culture decades after they are gone—unless people forget them.

In the same way, toxic past leadership leaves a scar that must be faced, not ignored.

In Communities

We drink from wells we didn't dig.
We stand on ground tilled by others.
We live in systems built by hands we will never know.

Some of that history is beautiful.
Some of it is painful.
All of it is instructive.

Even injustice and oppression, when remembered, can become catalysts for a better future.

Pamana teaches us:

Transformation is not invention.
Transformation is remembrance.

UNGGNO—THE PRESENT

If Pamana is the roots, Unggno (*uhn-go*) is the breath.

Unggno means to share the breath of life—to enter a moment fully, without ego and without separation, human to human. In Filipino and Pacific Island cultures, breath is sacred. You cannot fake your breath. And when you share it, you are committing to yourself and the other to be fully present.

Unggno can mean to "get rid of boundaries," or to "get close and become."

Modern science agrees. Emotional intelligence research shows that people feel seen not by what we say, but by the quality of our presence. Co-regulation—the nervous systems of two people calming each other—builds psychological safety. Teams with leaders who practice present, attentive connection have higher trust, higher performance, and lower turnover.

Unggno is the psychology of presence wrapped in ancient practice.

It is the opposite of multitasking.
The opposite of performance.
The opposite of leadership-as-image.

Unggno is putting the phone down when your child walks in the room.
Unggno is the manager who turns the chair toward the employee
instead of toward the laptop.
Unggno is listening—really listening—without preparing the
next sentence.

Unggno is how transformation feels before it is measured.

I saw this firsthand when we changed the way leaders began our sessions—
not with updates, agendas, or metrics—but with humanity.

Breathing.
Eye contact.
Gratitude.
Real check-ins.

Not the "how's everyone doing?" kind.
The *real* kind.

At first, people resisted. It felt too simple. Too vulnerable. Too human. But
soon, it became the most important part of every session.

And things began to change:

- Walls lowered
- Judgment softened
- Listening deepened
- Connection became real

**Transformation cannot take root anywhere if people are not ful-
ly present.**

Distraction is one of the most powerful forces preventing transformation in modern culture.

Unggno brings us back to ourselves—and back to each other.

KAPWA—THE FUTURE

Kapwa (*kah-pwah*) is one of the most beautiful ideas in Filipino psychology.

It means shared identity. **I am who I am in relation to.**
There is no "me" without "we." No "leader" without "people."
No "community" without "neighbors."

Western cultures often believe the opposite:

- "Be independent."
- "Stand on your own."
- "Pull yourself up."

But modern research echoes what Indigenous cultures have always understood: **transformation doesn't happen in isolation.**

The longest-running study on human flourishing at Harvard found that the best predictor of a meaningful, healthy life isn't wealth, success, or intelligence—it's the quality of our relationships.

Neuroscience shows the same pattern. When people face stress while holding someone's hand, the brain literally calms. When they face it alone, the threat centers ignite.

We are **wired** for connection.

We learn faster, heal deeper, and change more sustainably when we are supported—not when we stand alone.

Kapwa is the belief that the future is not built alone. It is **co-authored.** This changes leadership entirely.

Instead of asking: **"How do I get people to follow or buy in?"**

Kapwa asks: **"What are we, and what must we become together?"**

This is why teams achieve more when belonging is strong. This is why communities rebuild after tragedy through unity, not policy. This is why transformation spreads through connection, not control.

Organizations get this wrong constantly. They create mission statements, values, and goals—but forget that people don't transform because of documents.

People transform because of belonging. Kapwa is belonging embodied.

Culture of One Is Not About the Individual

The name confuses people at first glance.

Culture of One does **not** mean "everyone does their own thing." It does not elevate the individual over the group.

It means something deeper: **each person holds the power to catalyze transformation—right now.**

Not someday. Not when conditions are perfect. Not when others change. But **now.**

One person. One choice. One act of presence.
One gesture of dignity. One moment of courage.

Some of the most transformational moments we experienced were not the result of grand strategies. They were the result of one person choosing humanity when it would have been easier not to.

- One pastor apologizing publicly.
- One CEO crying in front of others for the first time.
- One educator telling the truth.
- One business owner saying, "I never saw my employees as people before. I do now."

Transformation always starts with one. And then? **It spreads.**

Neuroscience calls this *emotional contagion*—how the nervous systems of human beings synchronize.

Social psychology calls it *collective efficacy*—the idea that belief spreads inside groups.

Indigenous wisdom calls it *Kapwa*—the shared identity between us.

We saw this again and again. In rooms. In meetings.
Across organizations. Across an entire city.

Culture of One was not theory. It was a lived reality.

Why This Matters Before the 7 Conditions

Without Culture of One, the 7 Conditions would have remained separate ideas.

Our discovery revealed the power of their **sequence** and **connection** throughout the journey of transformation.

Culture of One awakens the possibility of transformation. The 7 Conditions make transformation practical, repeatable, and sustained.

- **Purpose** gives us meaning from Pamana.
- **Commitment** anchors us in Unggno—showing up, even when it's hard.
- **Common Language** becomes the shared identity of Kapwa.
- **Vulnerability** opens the Vā—allowing truth to breathe.
- **Consistency** takes transformation out of inspiration and into habit.
- **Deep and Trusting Relationships** form the human foundation of change.
- **Safe Space to Learn and Practice** makes transformation sustainable, not seasonal.

Culture of One is the light. The 7 Conditions are the lamp.
Culture of One is the breath. The 7 Conditions are the lungs.
Culture of One is the soul. The 7 Conditions are the structure.

Culture of One explains **why** transformation is possible.
The 7 Conditions explain **how** transformation becomes lived.

But here is the part most people miss:

Culture of One is not only the catalyst, it is also the outcome.

When the 7 Conditions are applied long enough, consistently enough, and intentionally enough, Culture of One emerges more and more naturally.

- Organizations begin honoring their Pamana.
- People practice Kapwa—building futures together, not separately.
- Leaders breathe Unggno—creating space where humanity replaces performance and belonging replaces fear.

At first, this starts as a choice.
Then it becomes a habit.
Eventually, it becomes identity.

That means:

- When Purpose is lived long enough, people stop asking, "Why are we here?"
- When Commitment becomes ingrained, people show up even on the hard days.
- When Common Language takes root, teams stop competing and start connecting.
- When Vulnerability is normalized, truth shows up without being forced.
- When Consistency becomes rhythm, transformation stops being an event.
- When Deep and Trusting Relationships exist, conflict strengthens instead of destroys.
- When Safe Space to Learn and Practice is built, failure becomes fuel, not fear.

The result? **Culture of One.**

Not individualism—but integration.
Not isolation—but belonging.
Not inspiration—but transformation.

It is both the beginning and the end of the journey.

- You start with Culture of One because transformation must feel possible.
- You end with Culture of One because transformation must become natural.

Culture of One gives us the language to see transformation. The 7 Conditions give us the structure to sustain it.

Together, they make transformation lived—not imagined.

Becoming One

Transformation begins when you remember who you are—and who you've always been connected to.

You are not standing on empty ground.
You are standing on Pamana.

You are not navigating this alone.
You are breathing Unggno.

You are not building the future from scratch.
You are becoming it through Kapwa.

This is what Culture of One teaches:

You are enough. Your community is enough.
Your organization is enough. Your people are enough. Your story is enough.

Everything you need for transformation is already here.
But remembering is not enough.

Transformation requires intention.

- Intention to honor the past
- Intention to be present now
- Intention to build the future together

This is where the 7 Conditions meet Culture of One.

They take the philosophy and make it concrete.
They take the story and make it a system.
They take hope and turn it into habit.

Most leadership books tell you what transformation is.
Most programs tell you why it matters.
Very few show you **how** to live it.

The 7 Conditions are the **how.**

They will help you build the habits, systems, and culture that allow transformation to happen—not once, but continually. They will teach you what we learned only through years of real work, in real communities, with real stakes. They will help you stop hoping for transformation... and start catalyzing it.

Because transformation is not magic.
It is choice. It is practice. It is breath. And eventually—**it is culture.**
Welcome to the journey.

Reflection

PAMANA—THE PAST

What parts of your personal or family story have shaped who you are today?

____

____

Whose sacrifices or lessons form the "soil" you're standing on?

____

____

____

What part of your past needs to be honored, remembered, or integrated before you move forward?

____

____

____

UNGGNO—THE PRESENT

Where in your life are you only half-present—and who is affected by that?

____

____

____

What would it look like to bring full presence (Unggno) into one relationship this week?

What performance or habit is getting in the way of real connection?

KAPWA—THE FUTURE

Who are the people you are becoming your future with?

Where are you trying to transform alone when you need support?

How do you want others to feel in your presence—and what needs to
change to make that real?

Commitment
Safe Space
Common Language
Purpose
Trusting Relationships
Vulnerability
Consistency

PRIMING FOR THE 7 CONDITIONS

What do you currently believe each of the 7 Conditions means?

____

____

____

____

Which condition feels most natural to you—and which feels most uncomfortable?

____

____

____

Where in your life do you most desire transformation, not just change?

____

____

____

Commitment
Common Language
Safe Space
Purpose
Trusting Relationships
Vulnerability
Consistency

Chapter *Five:*
YOU CAME FROM SOMETHING— NOW BECOME SOMETHING

The first time I heard that my grandmother once tried to take her own life, I momentarily stopped breathing.

The woman I knew—Lola, the matriarch of our family, the 91-year-old who still teaches at a university, walks 10,000 steps a day, and beats my son in driveway basketball—had once attempted to end it all.

I was sitting beside my dad on the couch, trying to process the words he had just said. Tears filled his eyes before they filled mine. It didn't make sense. How could the most purpose-driven person I've ever known have once lost the will to live?

That day changed the way I thought about purpose forever.

To understand the woman she became and is today, you must understand what she came from. And before I could understand what it meant to become something, I had to remember what I came from—a lineage shaped by both beauty and brutality, by faith and survival.

Where Lola Came From

During World War II, as the Japanese occupied the Philippines and the war neared its end, the Manila Massacre unfolded. Hundreds of thousands of Filipino men, women, and children were brutally killed at the hands of Japanese soldiers. My grandma, who was then only a young girl, lived just a few miles from one of the largest massacre sites. Experiences like that shape a child forever. Very few of us grow up within miles of such horror and survive—yet she did. And that reality is a testament to the resilience forged in her at an early age, the same resilience that would later ignite the deep sense of purpose that, in many ways, saved her life.

She has lived an incredible life since that horrific season. Let me tell you about her.

Lola is an immigrant to this country. Her legacy branches out through her ten children, thirty-four grandchildren, forty-six great-grandchildren, and two great-great-grandchildren, with more sure to come. Even now, she continues to contribute, teaching Filipino history and Tagalog as the oldest member of a large university's teaching faculty. Remarkably, she takes zero medication and, as I mentioned previously, consistently achieves nearly 10,000 steps a day—a testament to how driven she is to live.

Lola is revered by our family—a matriarch who is special to every single person she knows. Her impact has been felt by thousands, particularly in her early years in this country when she tirelessly supported countless Filipinos immigrating to the U.S. Each time I visited her home as I was growing up, there were often new faces living in her basement. They weren't my biological aunts and uncles, but that's precisely what I called them, which reflected the deep bonds she fostered.

She is an amazing cook, a talent that once led her to own her own restaurant. Her linguistic skills have also been invaluable; she has translated worldwide events from English to Tagalog and even served as a senior missionary for her church.

In her recent years, she has graced my family with her presence countless times. You'll find her outside, engaging in spirited games of basketball with my son in the driveway, taking my youngest on leisurely walks around the lake, or out on the boat with the family. There truly seems to be nothing Lola cannot do.

And did I mention she has accomplished all these extraordinary feats entirely on her own?

WHAT SHE CARRIED ALONE

Long before I was born, she and my grandfather—whom I only met a few times before he passed away—were divorced. It was a difficult divorce, from what I had been told. I knew my grandfather, Lolo, was once a good man with many great qualities, but, truthfully, I grew up not very fond of him for two reasons: he wasn't in my life, and I didn't like what I'd "heard" he'd done to my grandmother.

Now, as an adult, I long to be with him, meet him, and learn from him. Like many of my family members, I have moved past his wrongs and have learned to see him through love. Perhaps in the next life, I will have the opportunity to know him.

Back to Lola.

She remarried once during my teenage years, but that marriage was short-lived; her husband passed away soon after. That union gave her three stepchildren and multiple step-grandchildren, adding to the legacy I've already described.

All of this to say, my Lola has lived a life full of purpose, connection, and love. And if you were to ask her today what drives her, she would tell you it's her family, her desire to live as long as possible, and her wonderful relationships. She is determined to live as long as she wants—and I believe her.

It doesn't take a group of experts to look at Lola's life and realize that this woman lives with deep and meaningful purpose.

But why? How does someone find such purpose—and live it for so many years?

When Purpose Meets Pain

Lola has always inspired me, but I had never asked why she was the way she was.

The greatest purpose often grows out of the deepest pain. As Viktor Frankl taught, suffering brings about the deepest and most lasting form of meaning.

As I studied purpose, suffering, and human psychology, I became intrigued with why my Lola lived this way. Beyond the normal pain human beings endure, I wondered about hers.

So, I sought to find out.
And what I learned shook me.
In fact, it devastated me.

A few years ago, while grappling with the perplexing nature of Lola's life—and deep into my own research about meaning and purpose—I found myself talking with my father. In Filipino culture, he carries the significant weight of patriarchal responsibility as the eldest son. What I needed to learn had to come from him: the one entrusted to share his parents' legacy with me.

I was trying to understand Lola better and asking him why she was the way she was, yearning to learn about her past. (Modern Filipinos can be very private; sharing personal matters is not typical.) He humbly answered my questions and shared standard events I was already aware of.

Then he reluctantly recounted something that floored me completely.

During the most difficult period for my Lola—amidst the divorce, my grandfather's affair, the lies, the deception, the abuse, and everything else that came with it—things became so unbearable that she attempted to take her own life.

What?

The thought echoed in my mind. I couldn't process it. For a moment, I even wondered whether my father was exaggerating the truth. But then I saw a man who rarely shows emotion wiping tears away.

Tears welled up in my own eyes.

I couldn't reconcile how this remarkable woman—who lived with such profound purpose—had once reached a point where ending her life seemed like the answer.

Adding to the shock was the realization that there was a very real chance I might never have had a grandmother in this life—a woman who has long outlived all my other grandparents.

The multitude of memories I cherish... the chance to know her at all... might never have existed.

THE PROMISE I MADE

I sat there, tears streaming, my dad beside me, absorbing this entirely new piece of Lola's story.

While on a philosophical level, her deep purpose suddenly made sense, the emotional weight was overwhelming.

That day, I made a solemn promise to myself:
I would live my purpose more deeply.

I would etch it onto my heart the way she etched hers onto her heart. And I would dedicate part of my life to honoring her incredible legacy.

Lola is the ultimate example of living with purpose.
She reminds me every day that:

I came from something—and now I am to become something.

What can we make of this story?

Purpose Born in Suffering

Purpose can be discovered in many ways. Through our family, our faith, our work, etc. However, there is something about suffering that either refines or discovers the deepest form of meaning and purpose.

Purpose, in its truest form, often rises from the ashes of what was almost lost. My Lola's life is proof that meaning doesn't come after suffering—it emerges through it. Frankl taught that those who have a "why" to live can bear almost any "how." My grandmother lived that truth long before I ever read Frankl's words. She didn't search for purpose in books or seminars; she became purpose through survival, through faith, through the stubborn act of continuing, no matter what.

The ultimate gift, perhaps the most profound journey anyone can undertake, is the process of discovering and embracing one's true purpose—the truest form of oneself. I used to think becoming was a linear climb toward achievement, but now I understand that it's a rollercoaster of sorts, full of peaks and valleys. It moves through darkness before it reaches light. Becoming isn't about success; it's about returning to the source of what made you and allowing it to live through you again. Often, the valleys are dark, muddy, and difficult to see in. Yet it is where we derive the most meaning. My friend and author, Davin Salvagno, told me, upon meeting him for the first time, *"out of our pain we find the deepest purpose."*

Lola's story teaches that suffering and purpose are not opposites—they are companions. Her pain did not erase her; it refined her. What could have destroyed her instead transformed her into a living symbol of hope, discipline, and joy.

That is the paradox of purpose: it's born not in comfort, but in discomfort.

I often say to groups I speak to: "Discomfort is the cheat code to growth." That said, there are certainly variances in discomfort. There is discomfort we seek out to learn and grow from, and there is extreme discomfort not of our choosing, like what Lola experienced. However, our reaction to them can be constant and true—we can choose to embrace the discomfort, learn from it, and find meaning in it. Remarkable people, like Lola, show us that we rise to the level of the weight we take on in life. There truly is no way of knowing the upper limits of that potential, and Lola is a testament to that, still living out a deep purpose with every breath she takes.

Consider the meaning of each breath you take when you have been so close to not breathing at all.

Sometimes our life can only be understood in review of it backwards through reflection. But we can only ever live our life forward. As I stated in the introduction, reflection can be a superpower. But as Culture of One teaches us, the combination of reflecting on the past and building for the future can help us live with purpose in the present. Looking back, I see how Lola's moments of despair carved out the capacity for empathy and joy, and how her solitude created space for others to belong. That is now a defining characteristic: she helps others feel like they belong. The meaning of her suffering is not found in the suffering itself—it's found in what she built because of it.

When you think about purpose now, no longer imagine it as a destination. Purpose is not discovered in the mountaintop moments, but in those when you almost didn't make it. Purpose whispers in the same voice that says, "Keep going. Live one more day."

Our greatest gifts are often on the other side of suffering when we suffer well.

And maybe this is what it means to come from something. It means your story didn't start with you. It started with someone who chose to keep breathing when they wanted to stop. Someone who refused to let the line end with them. You carry their blood, their courage, their unfinished prayers. Lola is just one example in my life I chose to share; there are many others, countless in fact. We honor them by living today.

Purpose, then, is not something you find; it's something you remember. It's the inheritance written into your bones—the quiet agreement between you and those who came before: you came from something. Now, become something.

More Purpose in Action

You came from something—now become something. This is not merely a suggestion; it is the profound directive embedded in our very existence, a truth I've seen echoed not only in Lola's extraordinary life but also in the journeys of those I've had the privilege to witness and guide.

Hassan, who goes by H, embodied the "hard on the outside, soft on the inside" archetype I've encountered so often within the demanding ranks of law enforcement. For years, he navigated his career with a gruff exterior, a soldier in his own right, yet a quiet emptiness gnawed at him. He was a skilled officer, respected for his ability to maintain control and authority, but the "why" behind his actions remained elusive, a ghost in the machine. It wasn't until he participated in Groundwork, grappling with the concept of making his purpose bigger than himself, that a seismic shift began. He spent months on a deep, introspective journey, dissecting his professional identity, his role as a husband, and his responsibilities as a father. The sterile directives of law enforcement gave way to a beckoning understanding of human connection. Now, as an instructor in the Oregon Police Academy, H doesn't just teach tactics, he imparts the profound importance of finding deep purpose, of understanding that their badge is a vessel for service, not just power. He guides these young cadets through their own potential valleys of despair and doubt, urging them to see beyond the immediate and to become architects of something greater than themselves —a transformation I see as a direct testament to the inheritance of purpose.

This inherited purpose, this drive to become something more, is also evident in the story of the Dallas School District in Oregon, spearheaded by Steve. I remember sitting with their leadership team years ago, the air thick with the unspoken acknowledgment that their district's vision statement was, at best, a platitude—writing on the wall, as they say. Steve, then a school principal, felt it keenly. That day, he declared that such a void was unacceptable, that their vision should be etched on their hearts as it was on their walls —a beacon, not a footnote.

What he and his team later forged, "The Promise," was revolutionary in the world of education, an actual vision statement: *to know every student by name, strength, and need.* This wasn't a slogan; it was a living, breathing commitment. It permeated the halls, reaching even the janitorial staff, who saw their role not merely as cleaning, but as fulfilling that promise. One custodian, Carol, shared that her job went beyond cleaning the building; it was about helping every child feel seen and cared for. Later, we observed her living out her words.

Students affirmed feeling genuinely seen and cared for, which was a palpable shift in the school's atmosphere. The ripple effect was undeniable; the entire district adopted "The Promise." Later, Steve's engagement with our leadership institute illuminated a new layer of his purpose. Despite his proximity to retirement, he felt the undeniable call to do more. He applied for and was awarded the position of superintendent, and leads an entire district now truly dedicated to "The Promise" —a testament to how an inherited purpose, when embraced and expanded, can redefine not just an individual but an entire organization.

These examples—from Lola's unwavering strength to H's profound transformation and Steve's dedication to a district-wide promise—speak to the same fundamental truth. We are not simply adrift in existence; we are inheritors of a legacy, a tapestry woven with the courage, resilience, and sacrifices of those who came before us. To live with purpose is to acknowledge this inheritance, to understand that our lives are not isolated incidents but continuations. It's to recognize that the deepest meaning is not found in comfort or ease, but often in the crucible of hardship. That's where we are forged anew. We come from something—a lineage of survival, of love, of quiet determination. Our charge, then, is to honor that origin by becoming something that echoes that strength, expands that love, and continues that determination for the generations yet to come.

The concept of purpose, as I've come to understand it, transcends individual ambition. It is not a solitary peak to be conquered, but a shared valley to be navigated, a collective endeavor that binds us. Lola's life and the lives of individuals like H, along with the transformative work in the Dallas School

District, illustrate this profoundly. Since her deepest, darkest valley, Lola has spent her life giving to others. H's journey from a rigid adherence to protocol to an empathetic guide for young cadets, and Steve's relentless pursuit of "The Promise" within an entire educational system, reveal that true purpose requires us to extend beyond ourselves.

It calls us to build with others, to become interwoven with the fabric of their lives, just as they are interwoven with ours. This isn't merely a philanthropic notion; it's a fundamental aspect of our existence, echoing the Filipino concept of Kapwa, where the self and the other are deeply interconnected. Our purpose, therefore, should be a binding force, a guiding principle that shapes our actions regardless of our occupation, family situation, or any circumstance we face. While the expression of purpose may evolve, its core—its unwavering "why"—remains constant, offering a steadfast anchor amid the dynamic currents of life.

This foundational "purpose" is the bedrock upon which a life of meaning is built, a grander, more encompassing vision that fuels and directs the more specific inquiries of "why." It's the succinct articulation of what drives us, a set of values distilled into a powerful, memorable statement. It's no wonder that research revealed this to be the first and foundational condition of transformation. Without it, sustaining a journey of transformation is impossible. In the following pages and chapters, you will begin to see how every condition builds upon the next, starting with purpose.

I've often posed this challenge to leaders: *define your why in twenty words or less.* It's a task that appears deceptively simple, yet it probes the very depths of one's being. It demands introspection, a willingness to confront uncomfortable truths, and the courage to distill complex motivations into a potent, actionable creed. This exercise is not about crafting a grand manifesto; it's about forging a personal compass—a clear, unwavering direction that allows us to navigate the present with intention and build a future imbued with meaning. Without this clearly defined purpose, we risk drifting. Our actions become dictated by external pressures rather than internal conviction, diminishing the very inheritance of courage and resilience passed down to us.

The gravity of this pursuit lies in its ability to transform not only individuals but also entire communities. When our purpose expands to encompass others, when it compels us to contribute to something larger than ourselves, we unlock a power that can reshape the world around us. This is the essence of becoming—not a solitary ascent, but a collaborative construction. It's about recognizing that the legacy we inherit is not merely a story of survival, but a blueprint for continuation. By embracing our interconnectedness and understanding that our individual destinies are bound to the well-being of others, we can honor the sacrifices of those who came before us and forge a future where purpose is not a destination to be found, but a way of living that is constantly enacted, day by day, life by life.

Being Marked by Purpose

How can we make purpose permanent now?

The question of permanence—of etching purpose not just onto the heart and mind, but into a tangible, enduring form—leads me to consider the profound traditions of Filipino tattooing. For centuries, these intricate markings were more than adornment; they were a living testament to one's journey, achievements, and place within the community. They were a visual manifestation of a life lived with intent, a permanence earned through trials and triumphs.

The history of tattooing, or **tatak** (*tah-tahk*) and sometimes **batok** (*bah-tohk*), originates in the Asia-Pacific islands. Long before the modern world adopted tattooing as art or rebellion, our ancestors used it as a sacred language for meaning and purpose. It was how they told stories, signified accomplishments, and kept genealogy alive. Simple symbols held deep meaning. Each mark carried the weight of a life remembered and a lineage honored.

Tatak / Batok-
(tah-tahk / bah-tohk)
Filipino, "tattooing"

THE LANGUAGE OF THE SKIN: BATOK / TATAK

Among many peoples of the Asia-Pacific—Filipino communities included—tattooing has long served as a living archive. Marks weren't *decoration*;

they were ***declarations*** of lineage, vows, trials survived, roles accepted, and futures promised. A **mambabatok** (*mahm-bah-tohk*), a traditional tattooist, held a calling, not a job. Before ink touched skin, there were conversations—about family, place, purpose, and what must be remembered.

Common motifs carried shared meanings while remaining personal to the wearer:

Mata / Panyat (*mah-tah / pahn-yacht*)
Eye : vigilance, ancestral protection, the watch that never sleeps.

Filig (*fih-lihg*)
Mountains: journeys and the "climbs" of suffering that shape character.

Tao / Taomaru (*tah-o / tah-o-mah-roo*)
Centipede: people in girded unity—each "leg" an individual, all part of one body; also a protector of the crops.

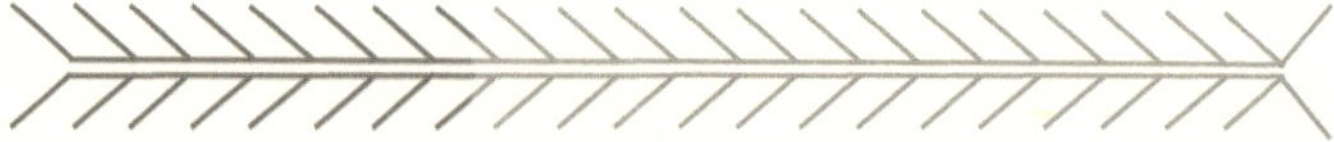

Ufug (*uh-fuhg*)
Kalinga hexagon/shell pattern: interlinked endurance; the loop of generations—arms linked across time.

Placement mattered. Sides, lines, and orientations could honor maternal or paternal roots, mark rites of passage, or signal responsibilities to one's community. In that way, tatak made memory visible: the past (*Pamana*), the breath of the present (*Unggno*), and a future held together in Kapwa. Being "marked" was—and is—a way of saying, I came from something. I am becoming something. I belong.

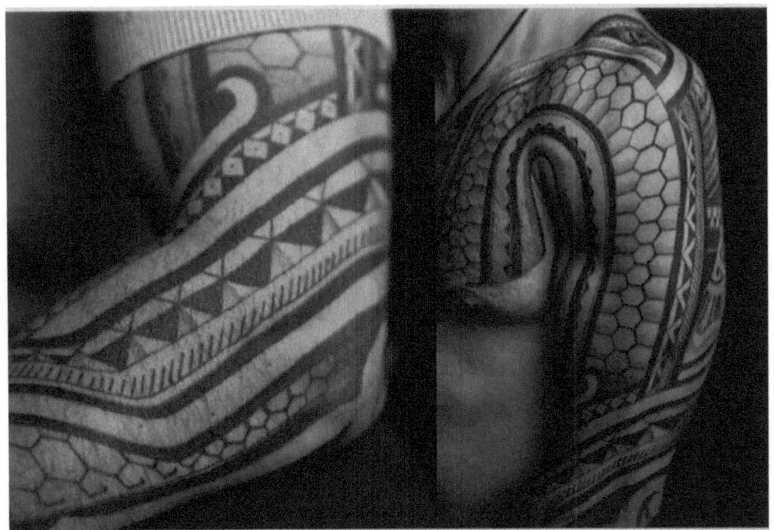

On my left arm and chest, I wear a traditional Filipino tattoo. Even the side of the body holds significance—depending on the region or tribe, the left or right side represents one's maternal or paternal roots. Across my arm and chest are motifs unique to my heritage, each tied to my deep respect for those who came before me. The overall theme is remembrance, transformation, and growth.

The Mata or Panyat—the eye—is on my forearm, representing the watchful gaze and protection of my ancestors. Inside my bicep, the Filig motif depicts mountains, telling the story of the metaphorical peaks—moments of suffering and triumph—that my lineage and I have climbed. The Tao or Taomaru—the centipede—winds through my arm and chest, a sacred symbol for the Indigenous Filipino people. The centipede, which protected the crops from insects and preserved the village's sustenance, symbolized lineage: a "girdle" of people, each leg representing an individual part of a greater whole. Tao literally means "people." The centipede reminds us that we are of one body, one community, one lineage—*Pamana* embodied in skin.

The most prominent motif on my body is the Ufug, originating from the Kalinga people of northern Luzon. The Ufug—a hexagonal pattern resembling a turtle shell or snakeskin—is one of the most recognizable Filipino symbols throughout the Asia-Pacific tattooing diaspora. Like much of Pacific tattooing, its shapes are drawn from nature —Earth and its creatures. My Ufug loops up my arm and arches across my chest, symbolizing the linking of arms and lives throughout time. It is an act of *homage*, a visual reminder that I am forever connected to those before me and those yet to come.

The Ufug is also the symbol that holds the 7 Conditions in this book. You may have already begun to notice its form—on the cover of the book, in chapter headings, in the flow from condition to condition, in the quiet repetition of shape and structure as the journey unfolds. This is intentional. The Ufug became both symbol and container for these conditions because of what it has always represented: connection across time, lives bound together, strength formed not in isolation but through relationship. In nature, the hexagon appears again and again—not by accident, but because it is one of the most efficient and resilient structures that exists. It is found where strength must be shared, where individual elements come together to create something that can endure. In the same way, the 7 Conditions are not meant to stand alone. They interlock, reinforce, and depend upon one another—forming a pattern strong enough to hold transformation.

The process of receiving this tattoo was unlike anything most have experienced, unless having also received a traditional tattoo. In Indigenous Filipino culture, the tattoo artist—*the mambabatok*—is not a mere craftsman but a spiritual custodian. As I mentioned, it is a calling. The title carries weight, reverence, and responsibility. When practiced traditionally, you do not choose your tatak; it chooses you—or rather, the mambabatok reads you. The process is preceded by conversations about family, purpose, and significance. Only then does the ink find its place.

Before a single design was discussed, I spent hours in conversation with my mambabatok. On the first of six sessions—more than forty hours total—I stood in his studio as he drew directly onto my body, freehand. No stencil, no replication—just wisdom, intuition, and ancestral knowing. Each symbol was chosen to reflect my story, my lineage, and my purpose. No other tattoo like it exists, nor will it ever.

One moment stands out vividly. During a later session, my mambabatok planned to ink a series of scorpion motifs along the inside of my arm—a symbol of the warrior spirit I wanted to embody. But as we spoke, he realized that my true strength lay not in aggression or defense but in connection and growth. In the middle of the ritual, he shifted the design. The scorpion became the fern—**pako** (*pah-koh*)—a symbol of life, posterity, and renewal. Remarkably, the two motifs differ by only a single stroke, a slight change in the angle of one line. That small alteration carried enormous meaning: my desire to protect transformed into my purpose to grow.

Pako - (pah-koh) Filipino,"Fern: a symbol of life, prosterity, or renewal."

This is what tatak—what being marked—means. Purpose refined through pain. Growth born through transformation. For thousands of years, cultures across the Asia-Pacific have literally marked themselves with purpose, inscribing their identity, struggles, and hopes into their skin. I carry this with reverence, honoring my ancestors and continuing the sacred practice. They will be remembered.

Your Mark of Permanence

For you, this is not a call to ink your body. Rather, it's an invitation to consider how you might mark your life—with permanence and intention. How will you etch your purpose onto your heart and mind? How will you honor your past, build for the future, and live each day with clarity of why?

I often engage participants in an exercise that makes this tangible. I ask them to make their purpose "permanent" for a day by writing it on their arm or hand with a Sharpie. This act, though temporary, connects them to the historical gravity of tattooing as an act of purpose. For our ancestors, a mark was much more than decoration—it was a declaration. It

represented identity, courage, belonging, and commitment to something larger than oneself.

This small exercise has a surprising power. As participants go about their day, they catch glimpses of their written "why"—a visible reminder of an invisible truth. It becomes a quiet conversation with themselves: Am I living this right now? When purpose is made visible, even briefly, it moves from concept to embodiment. It becomes lived.

When we recognize what these ancestral marks truly represented—the valor of warriors, the wisdom of elders, the resilience of survivors—we begin to understand what it means to live marked by purpose.

It's not about ink. It's about integration.

It's about allowing your purpose to shape your words, your choices, and your relationships. All of us, like Lola, are marked by suffering in some way. We may see these markings as scars, but through finding meaning in your suffering, those scars become beautiful symbols of your purpose.

As a keynote speaker and presenter, I've learned to expect two things. First, there are always individuals who feel moved to share words of gratitude after a speech—which I deeply appreciate. Second, not everyone in attendance will resonate with the message; there will always be a few who, for their own reasons, "check out."

That said, since I began presenting on purpose through the lens of Indigenous wisdom—inviting audiences to consider how they will make their purpose permanent—I've been continually amazed by the level of engagement. Rooms filled with hundreds of people are fully immersed, wrestling with their "why," working to understand what drives them. The impact has been humbling, and I have learned it is because scars of shame, regret, and trauma turn into marks of meaning, purpose, and becoming as they wrestle with my message.

After one keynote, a high-level leader approached me and said, "I was lying in bed last night, feeling overwhelmed and in a dark place, wondering why I'm here, why I even exist, and what I'm supposed to do with my life. Then I walked into the conference late this morning, and there you were on stage, talking about deep purpose. I needed every word of that message. I needed to find my why—and this has put me on that path. Thank you."

Encounters like that have changed me as much as they've changed others. Leaders have come to me afterward questioning everything they do—why they do it, even whether they're in the right career. Others have faced the pain of their suffering right there in the room, realizing that the path to purpose runs directly through it.

I've found that many leaders—though they hold strong values and care deeply about their work—have never been asked to articulate their purpose in a few words, let alone in one word or symbol. Many find meaning in their work, which gives them direction. They wake up, go to their jobs, fulfill their responsibilities, and feel driven by that sense of contribution. And that's good. But having *a work to do* can be taken from us. Jobs end. Responsibilities shift. Titles change. And when our sense of purpose is tied only to those things, it becomes just as fleeting as the circumstances of our lives.

So, what lies deeper? We might think it's relationships or human connection—and that's certainly closer to the heart of purpose. Our families, friends, and communities give us meaning that work alone cannot. Many people tell me their family is their purpose. On one hand, I resonate with that—my family is a profound part of mine. I find deep meaning in being a husband, father, brother, son, friend, and neighbor.

But on the other hand, even connections and relationships are not always permanent. Like work, they too can change. People pass away. Relationships evolve. Circumstances shift. Viktor Frankl wrote about this in his book *Man's Search for Meaning*. During his time in the concentration camps, he lost his wife, parents, and all close relationships. He learned firsthand that even connection to others, as profound as it is, cannot always sustain us—because it, too, can be taken away.

So, what, then, is lasting? What is the one source of meaning that cannot be stripped from us?

Suffering.

As I've already shared through the stories of Lola and others, suffering is not only necessary for deep and lasting purpose—**it is the only way to find it**. The meaning we discover within suffering is where purpose is born. No one can take our suffering from us; it belongs to us.

Consider the levels of finding meaning as follows: each level deepens our source of meaning and gives us a more lasting purpose.

First level of finding meaning = **Having a work to do.**
Second level of finding meaning = **Relationships and human connection.**
Third level of finding meaning = **Suffering.**

Suffering Well

While we shouldn't seek out pain, if we can learn to see it as a teacher—a sacred companion rather than an enemy—we begin to understand the eternal value of suffering well.

Suffering well allows us to extract deep purpose from the most difficult circumstances. We often try to avoid revisiting pain because it can trigger old wounds. But perhaps that resistance is a sign we haven't yet found meaning in it. I know this can be uncomfortable to hear, even triggering—but stay with me. If we continue to see our suffering as pointless, meaningless pain, we've missed its invitation. Both the suffering we cause ourselves and the suffering thrust upon us without choice hold opportunities for growth and purpose.

We don't have to romanticize it, dwell on it, or relive every moment. But have we engaged with it long enough to find meaning?

I've witnessed people do this—facing their pain courageously in real time. I've seen them take the invitation to be marked by purpose and find the strength to face their suffering, past and present, in ways they never had before. What once produced resentment, anger, apathy, or bitterness transforms into patience, understanding, and connection.

When we dig deep enough on our quest for meaning—deep enough to encounter our suffering—everything else changes. Suddenly, our relationships take on new depth. The work we do gains new substance. Our presence becomes more grounded, our "why" more enduring. Meaning through suffering is not merely part of purpose, it is the foundation of it.

It is here, in the furnace of hardship, that purpose becomes permanent—marked not just on our skin, but on our hearts.

As I have stated previously, being marked by purpose is not just the first of the 7 Conditions—**it is the foundational condition**. Without it, we drastically limit our ability to experience transformation on our journey. We limit our potential for becoming. And we risk forgetting the sacred truth of who we are:

We came from something—and now, we must become something.

The Call to Purpose

After weaving through the profound wisdom of Lola's survival, the transformation of H, the shared promise of Dallas, and the ancestral artistry of traditional Filipino tattooing, I find myself reflecting on my own *why*—the thread that has guided my steps through both triumph and trial.

My purpose, distilled through years of searching, is this: ***"To give my heart to God by being an influence for good and catalyzing transformation in the world."***

This isn't a polished statement meant to inspire applause; it's a truth I've bled for. It was not born in moments of ease but in the fires of adversity—through suffering, loss, and even the darkness of addiction. Like Lola, whose strength was carved from pain, I've discovered that purpose isn't something you find at the summit of life's successes—it's something unearthed in the valleys when you're stripped down to what truly matters.

Purpose is both a gift and a responsibility. It doesn't rest quietly in the background; it calls you forward each day. It asks something of you. It asks that you remember where you came from, who you belong to, and what you've been entrusted to carry.

And so, as you uncover your own purpose, I offer you these final guideposts, criteria born of both research and lived experience—markers on the path toward meaning that endures.

1.　**Purpose Is Discovered in the Fires of Adversity**
　　Pamana – Remember the Past

Every lasting purpose I've ever encountered has been forged in hardship. Suffering, when faced with courage, becomes sacred soil. My own story—and Lola's before me—reminds me that meaning is not discovered in comfort, but through the remembrance of pain and the wisdom it leaves behind.

Your purpose begins with Pamana—your inheritance, your lineage of resilience. Look back with reverence. What have you survived that still speaks to you? What lessons have your ancestors, your family, or your failures whispered to you in the dark?

Purpose without remembrance is shallow; it has no roots.

2.　**Purpose Calls You to Something Bigger**
　　Unggno – Share the Breath of Life

A true purpose does not end with self-understanding—it propels you outward. It calls you to give, to serve, to act. Mine has led me to hundreds of leaders through Groundwork and beyond, to share what I've discovered about transformation and to breathe life into the journeys of others.

This is Unggno—to share the breath of life. Purpose becomes real when it moves from your heart into another's. When it stops being theory and becomes connection.

Ask yourself: Who needs the breath you have to give? Who will be strengthened because you chose to live your purpose today?

3. **Purpose Connects You to Others**
    Kapwa – Becoming Together

We may begin our purpose alone, but we never fulfill it alone. Every purpose finds its completion through connection—with others, with creation, with God. The Filipino concept of Kapwa reminds us: I am who I am in relation to you.

Our becoming is shared. The work we do, the love we give, the lives we touch—they all form a collective tapestry that extends beyond any single lifetime. Mass movements don't begin in masses; they begin with one person at a time, willing to connect.

Ask yourself: Who am I becoming with others? Who am I building tomorrow with?

4. **Purpose Must Be Made Permanent**
    Culture of One – Marked by Purpose

Purpose fades when it stays abstract. It must be made visible, named, and marked. I invite you to write your "why" in twenty words or less—simple, clear, and personal. And then, to go one step further, find one word, or even one symbol, that embodies it. Let that be your mark.

This is your tatak—your sign of remembrance. The way I carry my ancestors' stories on my skin, you must find a way to carry your purpose on your heart. Because when life grows uncertain, that mark will steady you.

Purpose without permanence is only potential. Purpose made permanent becomes power.

Purpose Statement Lab (10–15 Minutes)

Goal: Name your why in twenty words or less, then distill it into one word or symbol—your personal tatak.

Step 1—Gather (3 min): List five moments that changed you (good or hard). For each, note what it taught you.

Step 2—People (2 min): Who benefits when you're at your best? Write three names or groups.

Step 3—Verbs (2 min): Circle verbs that keep showing up—*restore, build, heal, teach, protect, connect, renew.*

Step 4—First Draft (3 min): Template: "I exist to [verb] [who] by [how], so that [impact]." Trim until it's twenty words or fewer.

Step 5—One Word / Symbol (3 min): What single word or simple symbol captures your statement? (e.g., renewal, a fern, a linked hexagon, a rising line.)

Checkpoint: Could a friend repeat it back after hearing it once? If yes, you're close.

Make It Permanent: A One-Week Practice

Day 1 (Name it): Write your twenty-word purpose on a card. Place it where you'll see it at wake and sleep.

Day 2 (Mark it): Put your one word/symbol on your wrist or hand with a Sharpie for one day. Notice when it changes your choices.

Day 3 (Breathe it): Share your statement aloud with one trusted person. Ask: "Where do you already see this in me?"

Day 4 (Align it): Identify one daily action that enacts your purpose in ten minutes or less. Do it today.

Day 5 (Refine it): Edit one to three words for clarity or punch. Shorter > longer.

Day 6 (Offer it): Serve one person specifically because of your purpose. Name the why before you act.

Day 7 (Anchor it): Choose a lasting anchor: lock screen, bracelet, desk token, or a small sketch you carry.

Repeat weekly until it feels like muscle memory.

When we live in this way—rooted in our past (*Pamana*), breathing life into others (*Unggno*), growing in connection (*Kapwa*), and marking it within ourselves (*Culture of One*)—we embody transformation itself.

We are no longer chasing purpose; we are becoming it.

So, as you come to the close of this chapter, I invite you to pause and ask:

What suffering has shaped me?
Who am I called to serve?
Who am I becoming alongside others?
How will I make my purpose permanent—visible and alive?

Write your answers. Let them evolve. Let them mark you.
Because the truth remains: *You came from something.*
Now, become something.

Reflection

What suffering or challenge in my life has become sacred soil for purpose?

____

____

____

Which of my ancestors' strengths—or my own past lessons—am I ready to honor and carry forward?

____

____

____

Who benefits most when I live my purpose out loud?

____

____

What's my twenty-word purpose? My one word or symbol (*tatak*)?

____

____

How will I make it permanent this week?

____

____

Commitment
Safe Space
Common Language
Purpose
Trusting Relationships
Vulnerability
Consistency

Chapter *Six*:
CHOOSE—AND THEN KEEP CHOOSING

"Go back to where you came from!"

I remember the sting of those words as if they were branded into the air—sharp, hateful, and unforgettable. The first time I heard their shout, I felt my whole body tighten. Anger surged through me. My little fists clenched, my pulse quickened, and the hero inside of me demanded justice.

The voice came from a middle-aged Caucasian woman at the front of a clothing store. The target of her fury was my father—a brown man, an immigrant from the Philippines, and the store's manager. I was sitting near the front where my mother had left me, waiting for him to finish his shift, when it all unfolded.

Initially, the woman stormed through the front sliding doors, furious about an item she appeared to have purchased previously. Dissatisfied with the customer service desk, she demanded to "speak to the manager." I remember feeling relieved.

That's my dad, I thought. Surely, he would calm her down. But as he came walking down the long aisle in the middle of the store, I saw her roll her eyes. When he approached—kind, professional, smiling as always—she only grew more enraged.

She doubted that he was even the manager. She mocked his accent, dismissing his English as "unintelligible." My father, steady and composed, continued to speak with calm courtesy, as though he couldn't hear her cruelty. I, however, heard every word.

Confusion gave way to fury. I remember thinking: Why would anyone speak to my dad that way? Why isn't anyone stopping her? What did he do to deserve this?

And then she said it with her finger pointed straight at his face—loud enough for the whole store to hear:

"Go back to where you came from!"

Something inside me snapped. I rose halfway from my chair, ready to charge her with all the force my small frame could muster. But then my father looked at me. Just one glance. A look filled with love, concern, and quiet strength. It told me everything: Sit down. Stay calm. It will be ok, son.

I sat back, tears burning in my eyes, watching as my dad de-escalated the situation with grace that still humbles me to this day. The woman eventually left. The store returned to its normal hum, which angered me almost more than the woman herself. I thought that another adult in the store, an employee, another customer, or someone should have intervened and given that woman a taste of her own medicine... but nothing. People went back to normal as if nothing had happened. My father gathered his things and we walked to the car in silence.

I was shaking—angry, heartbroken, ready to explode. But I waited for him to speak first. Surely, he would be furious. Surely, he would tell me what he really thought of that woman. But he didn't. He simply drove. Calm. Quiet.

Finally, I couldn't hold it in. I burst out, shouting words about this woman I didn't fully understand—words I'd heard on TV and in school, angry words meant to hurt, just like I had supposed hers had hurt him.

My father pulled to the side of the road and abruptly stopped the car. He didn't yell. He didn't scold. He simply said, "Stop."

His tone froze me. He turned to me, eyes glistening, and said something I will never forget:

"Chris, some people just don't see what you see—but you have to love them. Remember, that woman is someone's mother, someone's sister, someone's wife. Would you want anyone to speak about your mom or your sisters that way?"

I softly responded, "No." He told me he was sorry I had to see that, but all we can do is love. Then he got back on the road and continued driving us home.

I sat there, silent. I didn't fully understand it then, but I felt it—the weight of what he was teaching me. To choose well, to love, even when you have every reason not to. To choose compassion over hate. To choose understanding over judgment. To choose restraint over indulgence. To choose *commitment* over carelessness.

He didn't lecture me about race, or injustice, or anger. He taught me something deeper: to see people as people, even when they fail to see you the same way. More importantly, as I reflect upon that moment, he was teaching me to *choose and then keep choosing.*

That day, my father made a choice. Not once, but twice. First, in the store—when he chose dignity over rage. And again, in that car—when he chose to teach love over hate. His choice was not a single act; it was a way of life. I've seen him make that same choice countless times since, always responding to bias and injustice with humility and grace.

Many would say he should have stood up for himself, that he should have "drawn a line." And maybe that's true. But what I've come to see is this: his quiet resolve, his commitment to love when hate would be easier, changed everything. It shaped his children and now his grandchildren, and it will shape his great-grandchildren and everyone who has ever known him.

Even now, I can't claim to choose as well as he has; I still have a long way to go. I've faced my own moments of bias and anger. I've felt the sting of judgment and the temptation to strike back. But then I remember his eyes—calm, steady, resolute—reminding me that love is also a form of justice. Justice without love is hollow. Love without commitment is fleeting. The power lies in *choosing*, and then when everything in you wants to stop, choosing again.

My father's example taught me that commitment isn't built in moments of comfort. It's forged in the moments you have every reason to walk away from, every justification to give up, every excuse to stop choosing.

That's what this chapter is about. **Commitment—the sacred act of choosing and then keeping on choosing—even when everything in you wants to do otherwise.**

The Depth of Choosing

Commitment begins where comfort ends.

It is the sacred act of staying true—not only to what you believe, but to who you have chosen to become—especially when everything in you wants to retreat. That begs the question: What have we chosen to become? What values shape that choice? And have they been rooted deeply enough in purpose to sustain the weight of commitment?

When I think about my father that day, what he modeled was not passivity; it was mastery. His restraint was not weakness; it was strength anchored in something deeper than ego. He embodied a truth echoed through philosophy, religion, psychology, and Indigenous wisdom: the highest form of freedom is found in what we choose to commit to. You can strip a human being of almost everything, yet our ability to choose—how we see, how we respond, how we believe—can never truly be taken.

My ancestors endured colonization that sought to erase their language, practices, identity, and beliefs. Much was lost. But not all. Practices rooted in deep truth endured. Mano Po. Unggno. The symbols of tattooing. These carried meaning strong enough to survive centuries of erasure. They survived because they were chosen—again and again.

At its deepest level, commitment is purity of will—the alignment of what we value, what we believe, and how we act, even when life tries to pull those things apart. It's not a one-time declaration. It is the daily decision to keep showing up. To keep choosing love, truth, and purpose, moment by moment. When heart, mind, and action align toward one clear thing, we become anchored in a way chaos cannot undo.

That is commitment: staying true to who we said we would be, even when everything around us tempts us to forget.

Psychologist William James called habit "the enormous flywheel of society"—the unseen force that turns choices into character. Commitment works the same way. Not through grand, dramatic declarations, but through the small, steady acts that say, I will choose again today. Every time we align our actions with our values, we carve deeper grooves of integrity into the soul.

Viktor Frankl, whom I referenced earlier and will continue to reference, observed in the concentration camps that those who survived often did so not by chasing after an impossible comfort, but by staying loyal to a meaning beyond themselves—which, as we discussed in the previous chapter, is found deepest within suffering. Commitment gave their suffering form. It turned pain into purpose and chaos into direction.

Purpose and commitment are inseparable—each fuels the other.

Purpose gives us the why.
Commitment gives us the how.
Purpose inspires. Commitment sustains.

That is why, in my research, commitment emerged as the second condition of transformation: it must follow purpose. Without commitment, purpose is nothing more than potential.

Like purpose, commitment is born from remembering—from our Pamana, the inheritance of those who endured before us. When we remember their resilience, we carry forward their unfinished courage. We don't simply honor them; we continue them. Our commitment becomes a living manifestation of our remembrance—the good and the painful.

But commitment also comes from Kapwa—the truth that our lives are interconnected. Every choice we make ripples outward, shaping not only our path but the paths of those who walk with us. We may experience choice individually, but we never experience its impact alone. That's why choosing well matters. That day in the store, my father must have known his choice wasn't just about him—it was about me, about the onlookers, about the generations who would hear the story.

My son, Mateo, was eight years old the first time he heard me share that experience on stage. He cried—not just because someone treated his grandfather that way, but because he couldn't understand how Papa chose love instead of anger. Afterward, he said, "Dad, I'm upset, but I also feel good inside about how Papa responded." He began to feel the tension adults often forget: our choices echo. We are not isolated beings making decisions in silence. We are part of a web of impact. Our choices outlive us.

Commitment also grounds us in Unggno—the breath of life we share when we stay present. Commitment isn't only a remembrance of the past or a promise for the future; it is a practice of presence. Inhaling what life gives us. Exhaling what we can offer in return. Repeating that sacred rhythm every day in how we show up.

Think about how difficult this actually is. If I claim to value love—especially toward my family—then I must continually choose it in real time. Not someday. Not when it's convenient. Now. But who among us does this perfectly? None of us. That is why commitment must be intentional. It is the endless pursuit of choosing what is right, moment by moment, even when we fail at it. There is no value in choosing love if unloving was not an option. No meaning in joy without sorrow. No beauty in transformation unless mediocrity was available instead.

Transformation is beautiful precisely because transaction is so easy. Many people accept mediocrity as success simply because they don't believe something greater is available. Resistant to change, we rename our present condition as "good enough." But commitment invites us beyond that. It asks us to choose transformation daily—to push through the mud of comfort and find the deeper waters of becoming.

My oldest daughter, Eva, once taught me this better than any theory ever could.

Our family had been part of a Polynesian dance troupe, often performing forty to fifty events a year. Eva loved it—her friends, the culture, the dancing, the music. Their teacher, "Auntie," was a force—born and raised in Samoa, talented, respected, and direct. In island culture, respect for elders is non-negotiable. My kids were expected to show it, even when it was uncomfortable.

During one of the largest cultural festivals of the year—thousands in attendance—Eva had back-to-back performances between that and a long soccer tournament. She was already mentally and physically depleted. Her team had lost every game, most of them by wide margins, and as the goalkeeper, she was scored on over and over again—a weight any keeper knows is heavy to carry. Exhausted, discouraged, and sun-tired, she went straight from the field to the stage. During one of the dances, she made a noticeable mistake. Auntie corrected her sharply in front of everyone—so sharply that Eva was heartbroken for the rest of the afternoon. As a father, every instinct in me wanted to take her home. To protect her. To shield her. My wife and I even offered to let her sit out the evening fire show. But she chose to stay.

That night, as the fire knife and poi dancers took the stage, we worried she wouldn't go out—or that she might get hurt. She was always the first solo performer among the young dancers, but when her name was called, she didn't appear. Someone else ran out in her place. My heart sank.

But moments later, right before the older dancers took their turn, Eva walked onto that stage—alone—with confidence I had never seen in her before. She performed moves she had only ever practiced without fire. Difficult moves. Dangerous moves. And she did it flawlessly. The crowd roared. Auntie cheered her name. The entire troupe met her backstage with arms raised in celebration.

Eva didn't just choose once—she chose again and again, even after being embarrassed, exhausted, and defeated. And her commitment turned adversity into something breathtaking.

She taught me that commitment is a living decision. Moment to moment.

Commitment is not rigid. It is alive. It bends without breaking—like bamboo swaying in the wind yet never forgetting its roots. It doesn't demand perfection; it asks for participation. To keep choosing when the easier path is to walk away.

My father's quiet strength was not an isolated moment—it was the continuation of his commitment to something deeper. His values. His purpose. His faith. When he chose love that day, he wasn't just shaping himself; he was shaping me. And through me, he shaped my children—just as Eva shaped me through her choice that night.

When we choose—and keep choosing—we join a lineage of endurance. We join ancestors, survivors, builders, and believers who stood at the crossroads between fear and faith and said: I will stay. I will love. I will build.

That is the essence of commitment. To choose once is courage. To keep choosing is what creates a condition worthy of transformation.

The Practice of Commitment

But commitment is more than an inspiring idea—it is a hard, gritty, daily practice that the world's greatest thinkers, philosophers, and healers have tried to explain in their own way. And so often, we misunderstand it. We think commitment is a feeling, a burst of motivation, a declaration made in a moment of inspiration. But true commitment is not emotional—it is spiritual, mental, and behavioral.

As I've studied this deeply, I've come to believe: commitment is the bridge between who we are and who we are becoming.

Every step across that bridge must be chosen. No one can walk it for us.

The Stoics taught it.
Religious prophets modeled it.
Indigenous wisdom preserved it.
Modern psychology confirms it.

COMMITMENT IN PSYCHOLOGY

Dr. Angela Duckworth describes enduring commitment as grit—passion and perseverance for long-term goals. But perseverance is not merely endurance; it is a decision repeated a thousand times. That's what people miss. Perseverance is fueled by identity, not mood. We keep going because of who we have chosen to become—not because the path is easy.

James Clear, in *Atomic Habits*, put it brilliantly:

"Every action you take is a vote for the type of person you wish to become."

Commitment is simply voting for your becoming—over and over again.

COMMITMENT IN INDIGENOUS WISDOM

Western culture often treats commitment as individual discipline.

Indigenous wisdom does not.

Across the islands, commitment has always been relational—a responsibility lived with and for others, the land, the sea, the sky, and the heavens.

In the Philippines, the tradition of **bayanihan** (*bai-uh-nee-haan*) says that one person's burden is everyone's burden. When a home needs to be moved, the whole village lifts it. When a crop fails, people share. When someone suffers, the community arrives—not because they must, but because belonging requires commitment.

Bayanihan teaches this:
I do not choose only for myself. My choices strengthen or weaken us.

*Bayanihan–
(bai-uh-nee-haan)
Filipino, "to carry
together"*

Other ancient values reinforce the same truth:

Damay (*dah-MY*) – to carry part of someone else's suffering.
Alok (*ah-LOK*) – to offer or sacrifice something so another can stand.

In Indigenous culture, a good person was not someone who stood alone—a good person was someone others could depend on.

Even leadership was rooted in commitment. Pre-colonial **Datus** (*DAH-toos*), the term for chief, did not rule because of power; they ruled because the community chose them and continued choosing them. A leader who acted without integrity lost the right to lead. Authority was not permanent; it was renewed through commitment to the people. On my recent trip to the Philippines, while meeting with an elder of the **Bantoc** (*BAHN-dohk*) tribe, I was taught about this principle. **Kadangyan** (*ka-dang-YAN*): earned by the community, you then have a responsibility to take care of people.

All this reveals something profound:

In our culture, commitment has never been private.
It has always been communal.
And that is true today.

COMMITMENT IN SPIRITUAL TRADITION

Across nearly every spiritual tradition, the instruction is consistent:

- Choose ye this day.
- Walk the narrow path.
- Endure to the end.
- Faith without works is dead.

None of these teachings speaks of belief alone. They speak of commitment lived out repeatedly.

Commitment is not a contract we sign once; it is a covenant we renew every day. We choose—and then keep choosing. Faith is a choice we must make every moment of every day to believe not only in a higher being or something divine. But it is an act of choosing to live in accordance with that belief.

For many, faith and religion is the first exposure one has to this idea of deep commitment to something larger than ourselves and our own values. We can learn a great deal from the faith practices across the religious spectrum.

COMMITMENT IN COMMUNITY AND ORGANIZATIONS

The modern world teaches the opposite—that commitment is personal, private, and individual. But Indigenous wisdom has always known commitment is contagious. It spreads.

I've witnessed this firsthand in Groundwork.

Hundreds of leaders—business owners, police officers, school administrators, pastors, counselors, CEOs—chose transformation not just for themselves, but for their people and their community. They made a collective commitment to break out of transaction, to build places where every person matters and every moment has meaning. And because they kept choosing, even when their teams resisted, even when culture pushed back, even when comfort whispered "good enough"... their organizations changed.

Not because policies changed.
Not because slogans changed.
Not because someone gave a motivational speech.

Change happened because leaders kept choosing.

They kept choosing to see people.
They kept choosing accountability and truth.
They kept choosing transparency and vulnerability.

They kept choosing transformation—even when it would have been far easier to return to the old way.

Some of the most beautiful culture shifts I've ever witnessed weren't loud—they were steady. Quiet. Relentless. A leader choosing well over and over, until others did too.

Transformation is never an accident.
It is the harvest of commitment.

Your Commitment

Commitment comes after purpose for a reason. Purpose reveals *why* you are here; commitment determines whether that purpose ever becomes real. Purpose may awaken you, but commitment is what carries you forward when awakening wears off. Without commitment, purpose remains an idea—something we admire, talk about, and occasionally return to when life allows. With commitment, purpose becomes embodied. It moves from aspiration into action.

Purpose answers the question: *What matters most?*
Commitment answers the harder question: *What will I do when honoring what matters costs me something?*

This is why commitment is not a feeling. Feelings fluctuate. Motivation fades. Circumstances change. Commitment is the choice to remain aligned with purpose even when clarity dims, resistance appears, or the outcome is uncertain. It is how we protect purpose from erosion. It is how we keep becoming when the easier option is to settle.

But commitment does not live in isolation. It cannot remain internal and survive for long.

The moment we commit to something meaningful—to love, to justice, to growth, to transformation—we are inevitably brought into relationship with others. And this is where commitment is either strengthened... or slowly undone. Because without a shared understanding of *what we are committing to* and *how we will live it out together*, commitment fractures. It becomes misinterpreted, unevenly applied, or quietly abandoned.

This is why commitment must give birth to something next.

Commitment requires language.

Language gives form to what we have chosen. It allows purpose and commitment to be named, shared, protected, and practiced together. Without a common language, commitment remains private and fragile—strong in intention, weak in execution. With a common language, commitment becomes collective. It becomes visible. It becomes something others can enter, hold us accountable to, and help us sustain.

If purpose is the north star and commitment is the decision to walk toward it no matter the terrain, then common language is the map we carry together. It keeps us oriented when the path becomes unclear.

It ensures that what we mean by words like, *love*, *respect*, *accountability*, *safety*, and *transformation*, is not assumed—but shared.

In the next chapter, we move into that work.

Because transformation does not endure through aspiration alone. It endures when purpose is chosen, commitment is renewed, and meaning is spoken in a language we hold together.

That is where we go next.

Self-Assessment: Are You Choosing... and Continuing to Choose?

Here are five questions to help you assess your level of commitment—not in theory, but in life.

1. When discomfort comes, do I retreat, or do I remain? What happens when commitment costs something?

2. Are my actions aligned with my stated values? Would the people closest to me say my choices match my beliefs?

3. Where am I choosing convenience over purpose? Who or what pays the price when I do?

4. In what area of my life have I stopped choosing—because it got hard? A relationship? A goal? A personal value? A promise to myself?

5. Who is impacted by my choices today? And what story will they tell because of how I choose?

Take time with these. Don't rush. Transformation is a slow, honest conversation with yourself.

Reflection

You might write, journal, or simply meditate on the following:

When was the last time I stayed committed when quitting would have been easier?

____

____

Who has modeled commitment in a way that shaped me?

____

____

What did I once care about deeply that I slowly stopped choosing?

____

____

What promise do I need to recommit to today?

____

____

If my family, colleagues, and friends watched my silent choices—what would I be teaching them?

____

____

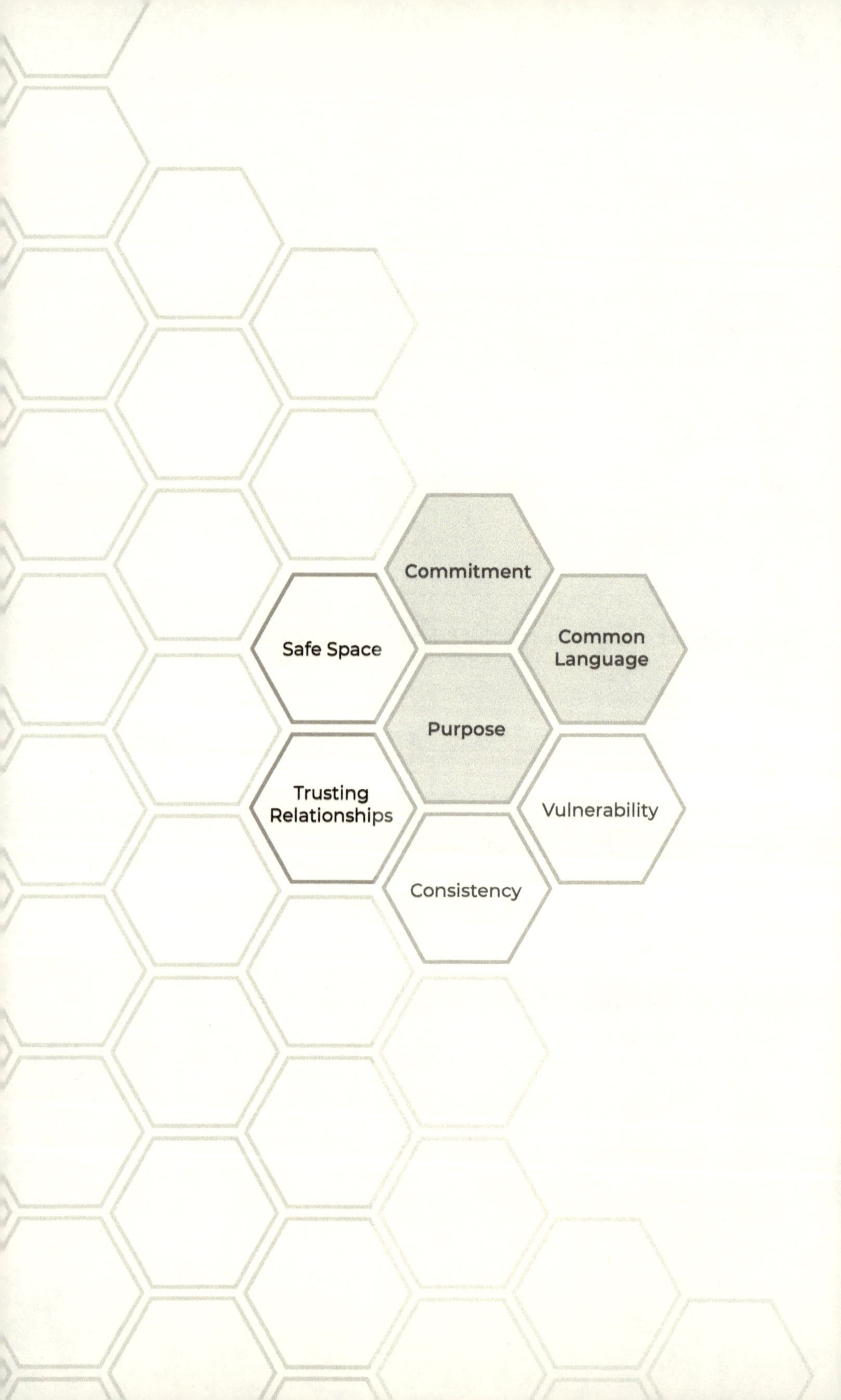

Commitment
Safe Space
Common Language
Purpose
Trusting Relationships
Vulnerability
Consistency

Chapter *Seven:*
DISCOVER WORDS THAT REMIND YOU WHO YOU ARE IN THE GOOD TIMES AND THE BAD

Words are the architects of reality.
We build our future with the sentences we choose.

In Asia-Pacific Island cultures—where my ancestry is rooted—language is not mere communication. Words hold spirit. Words create identity. Words shape destiny. In fact, many of these cultures did not keep a written record; history was predominantly oral—passed down through stories, proverbs, chants, key phrases, and metaphor. Our ancestors understood something modern society often forgets: speech is not just sound or a means of daily interaction. Speech is life.

And because of that, I want to begin this chapter with a man who transformed my life—not because of the work he funded, not because of his title, but because of his language. His name is Jason.

Jason is the son of the philanthropist who hired me years ago—the man who gave me the impossible assignment of transforming a community. But while his father gave me resources, Jason gave me something far more valuable: a way of seeing the world.

Jason has walked through his own fire—loss, fear, failure, seasons of invisibility, and moments of deep pain. I know pieces of those stories, shared in sacred confidence. What makes him remarkable is not that he has suffered, but that he has chosen every day to speak from a place of purpose despite his suffering. He chooses commitment each day—and he lives by his beliefs, both privately and publicly, inside of work and outside of it.

I learned that his power was not simply in what he believed. It was in the language he used to stay aligned with those beliefs. In a world full of noise, trends, empty slogans, and "flavors of the month," Jason chose words that reminded him who he was.

"Go Home at Five."

One of my first interactions with him happened when I was essentially offered the impossible job of transforming his community. My wife and I were sitting across from him and his business partner, Brian, at dinner. He didn't know me well yet—most of my communication up to that point had been with Brian. He knew me just enough to take a risk on me. So, I did what most of us would do: I tried to sell myself.

I told him I'd work hard.
That I'd pour myself into the mission.
That he could count on me.

He listened patiently, and then he cut through all of it with one statement I will never forget:

"Chris, I don't doubt you'll work hard and that we will accomplish great things together. But what matters to me is this: when it's five o'clock, go home. When you have time at lunch, take your kids out. Be present for your family above all else."

It stunned me.

No boss had ever told me that.
No one had ever said my family mattered more than what we were building.
And no one has since.

In most environments, it's always the job first, the bottom line, the business. Right?
Not with Jason. He meant every word.

It didn't take long for me to realize, after working with him, how deeply he lived by that belief. From those conversations, we developed a motto, one we repeated constantly in our work together:

God first.
Our spouse second.
Our children third.

We called it the "Big Three."

It became our decision-making filter.
It shaped our priorities.
It shaped our culture.
And most importantly, it shaped our language.

Because language is not just how you communicate with others; it is how you communicate with yourself.

Jason was never a mystery. I always knew how he would speak to me, how he would communicate with others, and I never worried about what he was thinking or saying behind closed doors. Consider how rare this is. Even in our closest relationships, we sometimes mistrust how another speaks about us—or how they speak about themselves.

Jason's language was not theory—it was rhythm. It was the air we breathed in every conversation. He would repeat the same phrases with a kind of quiet conviction:

Focus on the things only you can do.
Release control over outcomes.
Control only what you can control.
Let's help people find their own answers.
Let's be intentional.
What would we do if we had more faith?

These weren't motivational quotes or leadership clichés. They became the narrative that shaped how we lived, led, planned, and acted. While we were working on complex strategy—multi-sector partnerships, funding, systemic change—we rarely got caught in the technical. We stayed focused on what mattered most. And somehow, everything always got done. In remarkable ways.

I have also worked with leaders who use inspiring language publicly but abandon it the moment pressure rises. I have even worked with organizations that preached "family first," only to demand the opposite when the stakes grew. This contraction often leads to dissatisfaction among employees and contributes to turnover—not because the mission is wrong, but because the language spoken isn't the language lived. I share this not to criticize or disrespect organizations that have this problem, but to highlight something ubiquitous in leadership and organizational life:

Words are easy to say, and incredibly difficult to live.

As an executive leader myself, I have felt the dissonance of the language I put out into the world, not listening when I said I would, or not helping in a way that my proclaimed values would suggest. Leaders and institutions often love the language of values, but without a true common language— one that guides decisions in the hard moments—it is nearly impossible to sustain. Jason was different. His narrative never collapsed under pressure. His words and his actions stayed aligned, and that alignment became a model of what a real common language looks like.

Jason was reliable in his language—in serious matters, in spiritual matters, in business, and even in humor. Our mottos and patterns of discourse created a common language between us that I will never lose. And it started with his commitment to choose words that kept him aligned with his purpose.

At this point, I hope you're beginning to see how the 7 Conditions connect and build upon one another. They are different instruments playing in the same symphony—distinct, yet inseparably woven. Another wonder revealed by our research along the journey.

The Power of Narrative

Most people underestimate the language they live by. Jason didn't. He chose his words deliberately—not only in conversation, but in his self-talk, the internal narrative most people ignore. He used metaphors, analogies, mottos, scripture, philosophy—anything that would anchor him to what mattered most. None of it was temporary. It was a narrative—a way he made sense of the world.

When we met weekly—sometimes celebrating something extraordinary, sometimes grieving something painful—his language always did one thing: it brought meaning to the moment.

It *acted upon* what we faced, rather than letting circumstances *act upon* us.

Psychologists call this **narrative construction**—the way we interpret our world through the story we tell about it. It shapes the space between stimulus and response, which is incredibly difficult for most people. Many of us feel something and react instantly—not with a strong narrative, but a weak one, a natural one.

Jason was different. He made it a point to take control of that space between stimulus and response—to act upon it, not the other way around.

Neuroscience calls it **auto-suggestion**—the way repeated language re-wires our subconscious mind. There is a long history of research on self-affirmation and autosuggestion. In simple terms, it is repeating words—day after day—until the subconscious begins to believe them. The subconscious mind takes things literally. Carl Jung suggested that the subconscious is largely unknowable, but we do know this: repeated language can influence it. And when the subconscious shifts, the conscious mind—the part with logic, reason, and decision-making—begins to shift with it.

Behavioral science calls it **self-talk**—the quiet conversations we have with ourselves every day. For many people, these conversations are riddled with doubt, fear, shame, and self-criticism. These internal trenches hold us back and keep us from becoming who we are meant to be.

Social scientists call it **shared discourse**—the language groups use to create collective identity. This shapes families, cultures, companies, and entire communities. It is why Jason and I believed so deeply in creating a common language among leaders across sectors: because shared words shape shared narrative, and shared narrative shapes shared reality.

Scripture calls it something older and deeper: **"life and death are in the power of the tongue."** Not necessarily literal life or death—but the life of hope, faith, possibility, despair, fear, and resignation. Words can destroy a soul. Words can resurrect one. Words can start a war or end one. Words can break a heart—or heal it.

And Indigenous cultures call it something even more ancient: **words are breath. Words are spirit. Words create.** Across generations, Indigenous peoples chose words that would outlive them—words that carried identity, wisdom, obligation, and hope. Their language was meant to survive colonization, displacement, and change. It was meant to remind descendants who they were.

What a contrast to modern life—where our language shifts with trends, memes, algorithms, the latest news, and political cycles. We have much to learn from ancestral language—because their words help us remember who we really are.

We Talk Our Way Into the World We Live In

Throughout my years as a consultant, leader, and even conflict mediator, watching people talk to one another has taught me something profound. You learn a great deal about a relational and cultural health by the language its people use. I saw that people would talk themselves into a world that they could not talk themselves out of. It was as if once they got there, only action could get them out. Language crippled them and created a narrative difficult to change.

I began to see four kinds of narrative—four levels of language that reveal whether transformation was possible or impossible.

1.   Low-level Narrative

People talk about people. Complaints. Gossip. Blame. Cynicism.

This is the weakest form of language and narrative. It shrinks the world and makes victims out of everyone. It strips people of agency and imagination and immediately cuts off growth. Low-level narratives never lead to transformation because they deny the possibility of transformation.

2.   Mid-level Narrative

People dwell on and talk about the past—not in remembrance and honor like Pamana, but in resentment, bitterness, nostalgia, and even envy. This language attaches us to what was, not what could be. It keeps wounds open and creates apathetic people with limited potential. It buries potential under comparison and regret. Thus, generating a weak narrative, not allowing us the possibility of transformation.

3.   High-level Narrative

People talk about ideas, solutions, and a better future. This is rarer but certainly exists. This is powerful. People with this language see possibilities where others see problems. They use "we" more than "they." They talk about impact more than inconvenience and build up others.

Transformation begins here. Jason spoke this way.

4.   Elite-level Narrative

Almost no one does this. Elite-level narrative is when people don't just talk about ideas... **they execute them.** Not with frenzy or a checklist-driven transaction, but with meaningful, thoughtful action. *They don't just go through the motions; they create motion.* This language sounds different:

"What can we build?"
"What do you need?"
"Let's do something about it."
"I'll go first."

This is the language of transformation because transformation does not happen when we talk about change. It happens when our language leads us into *action*. Transformation is the journey, not the destination, but we cannot move on this journey without action.

Jason lived in the elite-level narrative. And that narrative became the foundation of Groundwork.

The Birth of a Shared Language

Before Groundwork was ever an organization, it was a conversation.

We believed that if we could bring together leaders from different sectors—business, education, government, nonprofit, and faith—and give them a common language, everything would change.

We called it the **5-5-5-5-5 Model.**
Five leaders—one from each sector— using one common language.

Why language?

Because we watched what happened when leaders all cared about the same problem, but couldn't talk about it the same way. Not to confuse this with diversity of thought—that is often good— but groups must have unity on key pieces: purpose, commitment, and a common language or framework.

One of the earliest examples of this was a multi-month effort to address homelessness in our community. Everyone cared. Everyone was united on purpose. Everyone wanted to help and was committed to making a difference. But their language betrayed their hidden assumptions:

- Business leaders saw economics.
- Nonprofits saw resource scarcity.
- Government saw policy.
- Faith saw scripture.
- Education saw schooling.

Same problem, same goals—**but no shared narrative.** So, nothing changed.

Truth be told, they were all correct in their vantage points, but unable to engage in discourse that would lead to change. Because without shared language, collaboration collapses into competing monologues.

This is not to say that conflict is bad. In fact, conflict is often necessary. It creates understanding, surfaces assumptions, and can lead to the best solutions. However, the **language we use to navigate conflict** determines the experience and the outcome for those in it.

In working with leaders/organizations and in my research, I began to see that conflict shows up in three forms:

1.   Task or Objective Conflict

Conflict around *what* we are trying to do and *why* we are doing it.

2.   Process or Procedure Conflict

Conflict around *how* we will accomplish the task—the disagreement on approach or style.

3.   Relational Conflict

Conflict rooted in personality clashes, offense, or resentment. This is where things become personal, and contention takes over.

The truth is, task and process conflict can be incredibly healthy. They can align people, sharpen ideas, and bring out the best in a team. Relational conflict, on the other hand, is rarely—if ever—healthy. It leads to distrust, defensiveness, and negative spirals.

And here is the sad part: Without a common language to frame conflict, task and process conflict often turn into relational conflict, simply because people start confusing natural resistance with personal attack.

This makes conflict bigger than necessary. It prevents solutions. And it keeps people from ever "catching" transformation.

This added to our realization that something had to change, and that's where the **Rooted Framework** was born.

The Rooted Framework: A Shared Language for Transformation

The story I shared previously in chapters two and three—about the fifteen leaders who shared the breath of life—was the moment all of our discoveries began to unravel. While we didn't have exactly five leaders from every sector, it was the beginning of business, government, nonprofit, faith, and education leaders finally being in the same room in a new way. And during that retreat, we introduced our literal common language for the first time: the Rooted Framework.

The Rooted Framework wasn't born in a classroom or a strategy session—it was born through ongoing, consistent conversation about transformational work. Long before Groundwork existed, Jason and I would sit together and talk about the problems we were seeing in our community. We needed a way to make sense of what was happening beneath the surface—why some solutions thrived and others failed, why some ideas took root and others died. So, we started using a simple analogy to guide our thinking—an analogy of land and earth: **Soil, Seeds, Weeds, and Fruit.**

At first, it was just language for us—our way of understanding culture, conflict, opportunities, and change. But the more we used it, the more we realized its power. As Groundwork began to take shape and leaders from every sector started coming together, that simple analogy became the foundation for something much bigger. We spent months turning it into a full curriculum: evidence-based, practical, and teachable. What began as two people trying to make sense of transformation became a shared language that entire communities now use to solve problems, build trust, and take meaningful action.

Here is a brief overview of the Rooted Framework:

Soil – the culture, the people, the environment. Soil is everything. If the soil is toxic—full of distrust, ego, fear, or apathy—nothing healthy can grow. No idea can take root. No change will last.

Seeds – ideas, programs, innovations, solutions. Seeds are everywhere. People have no shortage of ideas. But a great idea means nothing if planted in unhealthy soil. Without trust, belief, and commitment, a seed dies before it grows.

Weeds – conflict and problems at the root. Conflict, as discussed, is not always bad—sometimes we need to dig deep enough to uncover what is harming the soil. But most leaders only "weed whack" the surface. They address symptoms, not roots. And what happens when you cut weeds without pulling the roots? They grow back stronger.

Fruit – outcomes, results, success, or the lack thereof. Everyone wants fruit—performance, improvement, profit, impact. But fruit rots when the soil is neglected. Transformation is not about forcing fruit. It is about cultivating soil worthy of transformative outcomes.

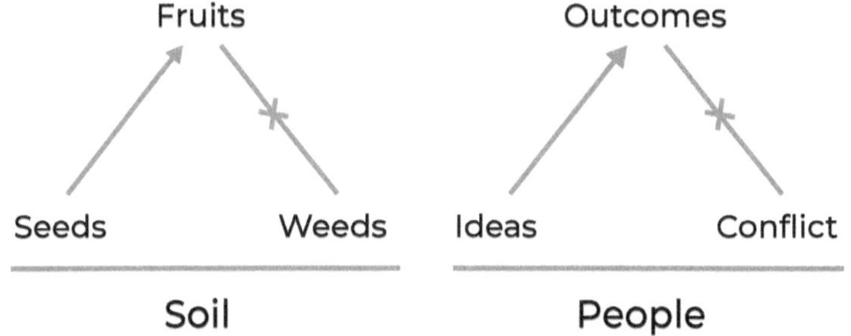

This is a brief overview of a framework that now takes hours to teach, supported by culture theory, accountability, relationship science, innovation, and conflict transformation. But what matters most is this: the

Rooted Framework became a common language, a narrative leaders could use together.

A language that could hold both the good and the bad.
A language that prevented and healed relational conflict.
A language that unlocked collaboration.

A language that helped an entire community of leaders remember who they were.

With this common language in place, everything began to change.

Remember that homelessness convening—months of meetings, big hearts, smart leaders, zero progress? After we taught the Rooted Framework, leaders finally had a shared lens:

- What is broken in the soil?
- Which seeds already exist?
- Where are the weeds, and how deep do the roots go?
- What fruit would transformation look like?

Instead of arguing over who was "right," the framework helped everyone become **one team**—not five competing systems. Once leaders had a common language, they moved from debate to action.

A great living example of this occurred with one group in our program who was assigned a seemingly overwhelming challenge: mental health. In each cohort we worked with, leaders chose a "problem of practice" they wanted to work on—a real, wide-spread problem in our community. The objective wasn't to solve it—its scope was too broad—but to workshop it using the Rooted Framework. They needed to analyze, understand, and problem-solve, and if this led them to action and specific ideas for engagement, we were in full support.

Huge scope. Deep roots. High failure rate.

Using the Rooted Framework, they spent months understanding the problem at its root. Starting out as a small handful of leaders across sectors, they brought others to the table, listened to their community, gathered resources, and began making actionable plans. Without us asking or requiring it, they ended up building something extraordinary: the first-ever Career & Technical Education (CTE) program in behavioral health for juniors and seniors in high school. When I say the first, I mean there is nothing else like it in the entire country that offers a credited CTE program.

Students receive hands-on experience in therapy settings, psychology, and mental health services—preparing a pipeline of future mental health professionals.

This program exists today and is bearing incredible fruit.

Not because leaders were smarter than before. Not because they suddenly had more funding. But because a **common language** gave them the ability to think, plan, and act as one.

That is the power of a common narrative.

Language can give our purpose life day to day and further help us live out our commitment to it. Whether it's one person trying to heal, a marriage trying to recover, a family trying to reconnect, a team trying to align, or a community trying to solve impossible problems. Transformation is not possible without a language strong enough to hold it. Without it, things fall apart. With it, people come together.

Indigenous Wisdom: *Words Create Worlds*

Across the Pacific, Indigenous cultures hold a sacred belief: *words are not labels; they are life.*

In Hawaiian tradition, language is spiritual breath.
In Māori culture, a tribe's identity lives inside its words.
In many Filipino tribes, to speak is to shape reality.

This is why ancestors carried chants, songs, and oral history with such reverence. They believed—and I do too—that language is the keeper of identity. When we move on, language remains. We do not simply speak words—**words speak us.** They form our memory, and they shape our imagination. They protect our purpose, and they call us back to who we are when the world tries to make us forget.

When I first met Jason, I was early in my career, yet I carried a big vision for myself. The purpose I've held in my heart, which I shared before, hasn't changed—it has only been fine-tuned. *To give my heart to God by being an influence for good and catalyzing transformation in the world.* I was committed to that but I hadn't lived enough to understand the value of choosing well, even when it gets hard. I lacked a consistent and solid narrative. I was ignorant, I was selfish, and I needed a frame for my purpose to be enacted. Jason gave this to me. He *was* that condition in my life. He gave me a "common language" that would serve me for years to come, both professionally and personally.

Though he would never seek these compliments, Jason is a profound example not only of this condition—common language —but also of a transformational leader at its core. Through him, I have catalyzed an endless journey of transformation in my life, and because of him, our community has seen transformation unfold in ways that only the language of those impacted can carry on.

Transformation requires purpose and commitment, but without language—words that remind you who you are—you will forget.

So, what about you?
What words do you live by?
What is your narrative in the dark?
What do you say when you're discouraged?
What sentences do you speak when you fail?
What beliefs do you whisper to yourself when no one else can hear?

Because in the good times and the bad, you are always being shaped by your language. And if you do not intentionally choose it, the world will choose it for you.

Reflection

Before you move to the next chapter, take a moment to write:

What are the words you use when things go wrong?

\
\
\
\

What are the words you need to start using to remind you of who you are?

\
\
\
\

What narrative do you want your family, your team, or your organization to live by?

\
\
\
\

Choose your words with intention. They are not a filler. They are not noise. Your words are your breath, your story, your alignment, and the architecture of the future you are building.

Commitment
Safe Space
Common Language
Purpose
Trusting Relationships
Vulnerability
Consistency

Chapter *Eight*:
OPEN THE DOOR THAT FEAR TELLS YOU TO KEEP SHUT

"I ran down the mountain that morning to save my marriage."

I want to tell you about the darkest time of my life. Truly, I cannot think of a scarier or darker period than the time this story takes place. I was newly married and living in Hawaii for school. My wife, Kenzie, and I had been married for less than a year. At first, we were in love—young love—and hopeful for a great life. But we found ourselves deep in the heartache of a struggling marriage. In fact, it got so bad that there were several days when I thought Kenzie was done... moments when I was certain she was packing up and leaving me.

Context matters. During this time, we were both collegiate athletes. I was at the peak of my game—playing well, receiving awards, and even being scouted professionally overseas. My major was something I cared deeply about. I was heavily involved in it and working in a coveted on-campus position, as the assistant director of a well-known center, gaining exposure to national and global projects. My mentor and boss, Chad, was a renowned specialist in his field, an author, and a sought-after consultant/practitioner. I got weekly one-on-one time with him, including extra-curricular early morning hikes he would invite me on.

On paper, my life was going extremely well—professionally, athletically, academically.

Yet it was the darkest time of my life.

My marriage was failing.
It was painful.
It was lonely.
And nobody knew—my wife and I kept it strictly between ourselves.

When we got married, one of the commitments we made to each other was to never bring others into our problems, unless it was professional help. I had seen through my family members that the act of talking to friends and family about marriage problems only added to the problem. In hindsight, we should have sought professional help. But my arrogance and pride—truly, my fear of being vulnerable—kept me from seeking it.

The dichotomy during this time was that I didn't know which version of myself was the truest reflection of who I was. The version excelling in athletics, academics, and work... or the version who couldn't seem to hold his marriage together, who couldn't make the most important person in his life happy?

During this time, I stopped praying.
I stopped studying.
I stopped "thinking" for myself.

I hated being alone with my thoughts.
Because being alone meant facing the reality I was living...
and I was afraid. Afraid to admit the truth.
So I avoided it—which meant I was avoiding addressing it with my wife and avoiding addressing it with myself.

One morning, Chad invited me to go on a hike. I had accompanied him a couple of times before—he liked to hike the mountain behind our town so he could meditate and pray to a beautiful sunrise. I relished these moments—talking shop, learning from him, deepening our relationship. Chad was so real—one of the most human-centered people I had ever met. He had incredible experience and was a giant in my eyes.

Despite his own struggles—which he would occasionally reference as teaching moments—I saw Chad as a hero figure. One thing I knew he struggled with was his own marriage at the time. He never shared this to vent or complain, but always as a lesson to help others understand the reality of life and relationships. Knowing this about him at the time somehow gave me comfort that I wasn't the only one.

I often wanted to open up and seek his counsel on my failing marriage. But my shame and pride kept me from telling him. In fact, he didn't know the state I was in until years later, when I thanked him and told him this story.

The trail was muddier than usual that morning; it must have rained the night before. It would take us thirty minutes to an hour to reach the summit—not an easy hike, but not extreme. As we trudged through the mud, Chad was strangely complimenting me the entire way up. Saying things like:

"Chris, you are incredibly talented."
"The sky is the limit for you."
"I believe you can do anything you put your mind to."
"You are one of the most gifted students I've ever had."

Now, don't get me wrong—hearing this from your mentor is flattering. But for nearly the entire hike, his encouragement continued. It quickly became uncomfortable; it felt excessive—like he was up to something—but mostly I felt unworthy of it.

While I was performing well in every aspect of my life, I knew deep down that I was failing in the most important relationship of my life. So, I just listened quietly, offering an occasional and bashful "thank you."

When we reached the top, the sun was cresting the horizon. Chad asked for a few minutes to go pray and meditate. I sat alone at the top of the mountain. Remember—I hated being alone with my thoughts. My mind raced back to the dichotomy I was living. I tried to distract myself with the beauty of the sunrise, the smell of the island air... tried to convince myself I was lucky to be living in paradise and sunshine, yet still feeling like darkness was consuming me.

When Chad returned, he asked if we could sit. We found a gnarly tree with branches stretched over the pathway, perfectly positioned like benches for us. It would have been the perfect moment to tell him the truth—to ask for help. But I didn't. Fear would not let me open that door.

Instead, he spoke.

He said, "I hope I'm not overstepping, but I feel like I should tell you something."

With a soft smile, he even pointed out how excessive his compliments had been on the hike. I laughed and said, "Yeah, I'm grateful, but it was getting kind of weird." He smiled—then grew serious.

"Chris, I know it might have been uncomfortable, but I want you to know I meant every word. I think you're talented. I think you can do anything you put your mind to. But this morning, I feel prompted to tell you something..."

I nodded. There was nothing Chad could say that would upset me. He was my greatest mentor.

Then he said:

"Chris, I don't know if this is relevant to your life right now. But you know my marriage has struggled—a lot. If yours ever does, please remember this: I believe you can accomplish everything I said.

But if you don't keep your wife, Kenzie, a part of everything you do, and if you don't stay a part of everything she does, I think you will only accomplish a fraction of your potential. Staying aligned with your partner is everything."

I was shaken to my core.

On the outside, I stayed calm. I quietly said, "Thank you, Chad. That's great advice."

On the inside, I had never wanted to change more. I had this bursting desire to open the door I had not only kept shut, but padlocked and thrown away the key.

Chad and I walked down the mountain together. In my heart, I ran.

When we reached the trailhead, I thanked him, said goodbye, and jumped on my bike, pedaling as hard as I could toward home. When I reached our little studio apartment, I ran up the stairs, left my muddy shoes at the door, and rushed to the bedside where Kenzie was still asleep. I fell to my knees, waking her with tears streaming down my face—begging her forgiveness and pleading my case that I would make things right, that I would change.

It was the first of many vulnerable conversations—many encounters with fear—that led to us transforming our relationship.

The mud on my shoes, left at the door, is symbolic to me now. It was fear—built up over time from my inability to be honest with myself and others. It was excuse-making. Justification. Finger-pointing. My shame kept the door locked. But that morning, I opened it.

I ran down a mountain because I realized no mountain was worth ascending if I was leaving the most precious thing in my life behind.

The Mountain and Muddy Shoes

I want you to think about two things:

1. Who or what do you need to run down the mountain for—because without it, you will not experience transformation?

2. What is the mud you need to leave at the door—the fear keeping it shut?

My hope in this chapter is that you will open the door fear tells you to keep shut—through vulnerability. I hope your organizations will tell themselves the truth about what is preventing their potential. I hope our communities will shed the calluses fear creates—barriers that distance us from one another—and become more vulnerable in the face of discord. I hope that in your life you can face the relationships that are currently beckoning for change, that need you to open the door first, even if everything is telling you not to.

To me, vulnerability at its core is telling the truth about yourself, first to yourself,—and then to others. This is a deep movement of the psyche and soul. It is not divulging private information for the sake of attention. It is intentionally opening your heart to others for the purpose of helping others do the same. Kapwa connects us and being resistant or reserved limits the potential of that connection and what we can do with one another.

While the conditions of Purpose, Commitment, and Common Language are key and tangible conditions on the journey of transformation, Vulnerability is the doorway that opens to the metaphorical leaps and bounds waiting on the journey. This is when we start to literally change—in body, spirit, and emotion. For many, I have seen vulnerability unlock transformational moments in the room. It is what people remember. It is what they lean on.

Unlike the conditions before and after it, Vulnerability is the only one that cannot be easily orchestrated.

Vulnerability is being most human in the space where we can truly meet one another. Amid Kapwa—of the Vā—it takes vulnerability to venture and "dare" to explore that space.

I am reminded of the Christmas Truce of 1914, where in the midst of trench warfare on Christmas Day, German and French/English soldiers dared to step into no man's land—to meet in the literal space between. They exchanged gifts, cut one another's hair, played soccer, and celebrated Christmas Day together. What started the night before with one side singing "Silent Night," turned into what must have been a beautiful sound breaking through the war-torn air as both sides sang Christmas hymns back and forth.

The vulnerability that started that night—little by little—led to someone taking the ultimate risk and venturing into no man's land. Many followed. Many celebrated. Many "saw" one another in that space between.

Søren Kierkegaard said that love is not an expression of the one who is loved, but of the one *who* loves. It takes intentional action and risk to be vulnerable. "What if they don't reciprocate? What if they hurt me?" At minimum, it feels uncomfortable. At the extreme—it feels dangerous.

But let me make this important claim:
Transformation was never a comfortable journey to begin with.

Transformation is born in the fires of adversity and discomfort—carried by the act and internal choice of vulnerability.

I have seen this space—like the trench warfare of World War I, full of metaphorical battle, disdain, hate, and anger—turn into something beautiful, like the Christmas Day truce. But it does not happen without vulnerability, the ultimate sign that transformation is occurring and possible.

For many soldiers that day, the act of venturing out didn't just expose their safety, it exposed their humanity. Some gave their only gifts—sent from family—to the very soldiers they were fighting. What a beautiful symbol. What gift can we give our enemies?

Our vulnerability.

They didn't run out there out of nowhere. It was intentional. It had parameters. It had context. Just like my morning on that mountain with Chad. It took vulnerability over time—his vulnerability with me about his marriage, the sacred space of being on a mountain, the sunrise, the quiet, the human-to-human conversation—for me to open a door I had kept locked.

That day saved my marriage. The truth is, both versions of me were the reality of who I was; I just needed to admit that in order to move forward. Everything I have now—my marriage, my children, my career, my joy— exists because of that morning.

It led me to leave my muddy shoes at the door... and transform into the man I am today.

Let's Discuss Fear

I want to speak to the cynic in the room—the one who hears the word "vulnerability" and immediately wants to shut down. The one who thinks this is touchy-feely, soft, risky, or unnecessary. If that is you, let me ask gently: *What scares you about it?*

That fear—whatever it is—is the very reason vulnerability matters.

Fear is not the enemy. Fear protects us. Fear has kept human beings alive for thousands of years. But fear also keeps us from opening doors we are meant to walk through. Remember, vulnerability is not oversharing, it is not attention-seeking, and it is not reckless disclosure. Vulnerability is not telling everyone everything. **It is telling the *right truth* at the *right time* for the sake of connection, healing, or transformation.**

If you are open to it—if you simply unlock the door—you will know when the right moment comes. You will feel the pull. You will recognize the invitation. But do not withhold yourself from transformation because fear is asking you to stay the same.

Vulnerability is also not conditional on the reciprocity of others. If you are vulnerable only as long as the other person responds a certain way, that is not vulnerability—that is manipulation. True vulnerability is unconditional. The first soldier who stepped into no man's land during the Christmas Truce of 1914 did not know whether he would be shot or embraced. He only knew something in him was calling him forward. His vulnerability unlocked the vulnerability of others.

And look at what awaited.

If I could travel through time, I would want to witness that morning in 1914. Two armies, covered in mud and surrounded by death, met in the space between. The night before, one side began singing; the other side joined. Little by little, fear gave way. By morning, someone dared to step into the open. That single act turned a battlefield into holy ground.

The dictionary defines vulnerability as the exposure of oneself to physical or emotional pain. But let me ask you honestly: *are you not already in pain?* Was I not in pain before I ran down that mountain years ago? Was I not suffering, afraid, and ashamed long before vulnerability ever entered the room? Yes. Vulnerability did not create the pain—it changed the direction of it. It gave meaning to it. It transformed it.

And think back to your work in chapter five, where we wrestled with purpose and the meaning found in suffering. Did any of that meaning appear without vulnerability? Absolutely not. Every meaningful transformation in human history—personal, relational, organizational, societal—began with someone telling the truth when it would have been easier not to.

The Psychology of Fear and Vulnerability

Fear is ancient. It is older than language, older than culture, older than reason. The human nervous system was wired to keep us alive long before it learned to understand emotion. When vulnerability feels terrifying, it is not because we are weak—it is because our biology believes exposure is dangerous. Neuroscientists explain that vulnerability activates the same neural pathways as physical pain. Rejection, embarrassment, being seen, loss of control—the brain interprets them as a threat.

So, our instinct to shut down, hide, stay silent, or pretend we are fine is not irrational—it is survival.

But survival is not transformation. Surviving keeps us alive. Vulnerability makes us human.

Psychology calls vulnerability a *courage-based behavior*—the willingness to act in alignment with our values despite emotional risk. Courage is not the absence of fear; courage is doing the right thing while fear is present. Carl Rogers, one of the founders of humanistic psychology, observed: "What is most personal is most universal." When we hide, we suffer alone. When we speak, we discover we are not alone.

Behavioral science calls this *reciprocal authenticity*—one person's truth unlocks another's. One open door opens others. And that is why vulnerability becomes a turning point: transformation stops being theoretical and becomes real.

In the research that revealed these 7 Conditions, Vulnerability was the most discussed, most emotional, and most transformative. It is the fourth of the seven—right in the center—because it is the hinge everything turns on. When the door remained shut, transformation stalled. When it opened—when someone finally told the truth—time slowed. The room changed. People changed. Vulnerability wasn't a side note; it was the moment transformation began breathing. Let me share some examples.

Sacred Ground

In our leadership institute and programs, everything is intentional. Intentionality fuels transformation. During every retreat or session, we created something we called "digging deep," similar to a biggest-takeaway exercise—two hours dedicated solely to reflection and truth-telling. After days of work, this was the moment where people chose whether to open the door or keep it shut.

At first, it was always silent. Always awkward. Always hesitant.

Until someone finally took the risk.

I will never forget one of those moments. A room of thirty leaders—CEOs, educators, nonprofit directors, pastors, civic leaders—from different backgrounds, ages, and beliefs. One man, a Black leader who had been quiet for most of the retreat, stood up and said:

"Two days ago, when I walked into this room, my first thought was, 'This group isn't very diverse.' I judged you. And I'm ashamed of it. I want to apologize. After three days with you, I realize this is one of the most diverse rooms I've ever been in—not because of skin color, but because of story, experience, and humanity. I'm grateful. I'm changed. Thank you."

In that moment, the room elevated. It was as if every person reached for the metaphorical key they had been holding and unlocked the door fear was guarding.

One leader stood and said he had lived in the community for years but had always felt alone, and that he and his family had even considered moving on numerous occasions. After this experience, he knew he would never leave. Another leader, a CEO, shared openly about her daughter—they had been struggling and every conversation ended in arguments or silence, but the night before, her daughter joked on the phone: "Mom, what kind of retreat is this? Because you're different... and I like it."

Another leader—one deeply involved in foster care and homelessness—said: "I carry so much fear about the future. Fear for my kids. Fear for my community. I lose sleep over it. But for the first time in a long time, I'm hopeful. Because I see all of you out there fighting for something better."

One by one, they unlocked the door.

This was not therapy.
This was not soft.
This was not forced.

It was transformation.

What began as strangers trading transactional handshakes ended with people who had *shared the breath of life* with one another—forming transformational relationships. It was a preview of Condition Six: Deep and Trusting Relationships. This is the difference between a handshake and the Unggno. One is safe and transactional. The other is vulnerable and transformational. And the difference in outcome is staggering.

When the session ended, no one wanted to leave. It felt like a holy moment, not because it was spiritual in a religious sense, but because human dignity had been honored in the deepest way.

I didn't know how to close it. "Thank you" felt too small. "Have a good day" felt disrespectful to the sacredness of what happened in that room. So, I did the only thing my spirit knew to do:

I removed my shoes.

Growing up in a Filipino-influenced home, we were taught to always remove our shoes before entering someone's home. In other Island cultures alike, removing your shoes is a sign of respect. People do it not simply for cleanliness, but to leave the "mud of the world" behind. In Samoa and Tonga, in Fiji, in Hawaii and throughout Aotearoa (New Zealand), shoes are removed before entering spaces made sacred by story, ancestry, or relationship. In Māori tradition, the **Marae** (*mah-rah-eh*) is the center of the village—the house of ancestors. Carvings cover the walls, each one telling the genealogy of the tribe. To enter a Marae without removing your shoes would be unthinkable.

*Marae -
(mah-rah-eh)*
Māori, "Center
of the village"

That day, as everyone watched, awaiting my next instruction, I removed my shoes, walked to the center of the room, and placed them on the floor. I told them why. I told them what it meant. I told them they had created sacred ground. Then I invited them to do the same—to go home to their families, their teams, and their community and create that same sacred space where vulnerability could breathe.

Indigenous Wisdom on Vulnerability

Hiya -(hee-ya)
Filipino, "Humility"

Across the Philippines, vulnerability is not weakness—it is dignity. The Indigenous concept of **Hiya** (*hee-ya*) is often mistranslated as shame, but before colonization, hiya meant humility. It was the willingness to soften oneself for the sake of a relationship. It reminded people that pride destroys connection, but humility restores it.

*Pakiramdam -
(pa-kee-RAHM
-dam)* Filipino,
"Deep relational
awareness"

There is also **Pakiramdam** (*pa-kee-RAHM-dam*)—a deep relational awareness, the ability to sense the emotional state of another without words. Filipinos are taught to feel the room, to notice silence, to respond to pain with gentleness. Pakiramdam is vulnerability as empathy.

At the heart of Filipino psychology, as I have referenced consistently throughout this book —and as a great example in this chapter—is Kapwa, the belief that the self and the other are not separate. To harm you is to harm me. To restore you is to restore me. Historically, conflicts in Filipino communities were often resolved through open apology and symbolic acts of unity because the collective was valued more than the individual. Vulnerability was a form of strength, not surrender.

Perhaps One of the Greatest Examples

In Samoa, there is a sacred practice of reconciliation called **Ifoga** (*ee-foh-nga*)—perhaps the most beautiful living example of vulnerability on Earth that I have come across. When one person or family has caused harm to another, they arrive silently at the home of the offended family at dawn. They kneel outside and cover themselves with Tapa (*tah-pah*) Cloth, a ceremonial-like fine mat, bowing themselves low to the ground.

Ifoga – (ee-foh-nga) Samoan, "Reconciliation Ceremony"

Tapa – (tah-pah) Samoan, "Ceremonial-like fine mat"

They do not defend themselves.
They do not demand forgiveness.
They place themselves fully, visibly vulnerable.

Their bodies speak the truth: *We are here in humility. We are willing to suffer with you. We are willing to be exposed until you are ready to lift the mat.*

Sometimes forgiveness comes quickly. Sometimes it takes hours. Sometimes the family weeps. Sometimes they wrestle. But the Ifoga continues until the mats are lifted, signaling reconciliation. Community gathers. People embrace. Gifts are exchanged. The relationship is restored.

This is vulnerability at its highest form:

Lowering oneself so another can rise.
Choosing restoration over pride.
Choosing humanity over fear.

Ifoga teaches a timeless truth: *Vulnerability restores what fear destroys.*

Open the Door

Hear this clearly: vulnerability is not weakness. It is not emotional chaos. It is not spilling secrets or chasing attention. Vulnerability is telling the truth about yourself—first to yourself, then to others—for the sake of transformation.

It saved my marriage. It changed my leadership. It changed my life.

I have witnessed entire communities—divided, distrustful, exhausted—become hopeful again because one person chose to tell the truth. I have watched hardened leaders cry at tables where they once defended. I have watched strangers become brothers and sisters because someone dared to walk into no man's land with nothing but courage.

You cannot have transformation without vulnerability.

Purpose gives direction. Commitment sustains momentum. Common language keeps us aligned. But vulnerability—vulnerability changes us.

So, I ask you:

What door is fear telling you to keep shut?
Who do you need to tell the truth to?
Where have you been hiding from your own heart?

Because you may not need to climb another mountain. You may just need to run down one.

Reflection

Before moving to the next chapter, take a moment to write:

What truth about yourself have you been avoiding?

____

____

Who do you need to repair with, reconnect with, or return to?

____

____

What is the "mud" you need to leave at the door?

____

____

What relationship, team, or community needs sacred ground—and what small act of vulnerability could begin it?

____

____

And one final question:

What might be waiting for you on the other side of the door fear is keeping shut?

____

____

____

When you are ready, turn the handle.

Commitment
Safe Space
Common Language
Purpose
Trusting Relationships
Vulnerability
Consistency

Chapter *Nine:*
DO ORDINARY THINGS WITH SACRED INTENTION

Transformation is a big word—one that makes most people think of break-throughs, lightning-bolt moments, glory, or dramatic change. And yes, sometimes transformation looks like that. Sometimes it's a mountain-top moment. Sometimes it's a Christmas Truce. Sometimes it's running down a mountain to save your marriage.

But if you remember how we defined transformation earlier in this book, it isn't always loud or explosive. Transformation is *a fundamental shift toward positive potential in how we see, think, or behave.* Sometimes that shift happens in a single moment, and we should cherish those moments as a gift. Most of the time, it happens slowly, quietly, daily. Not in leaps, but in footsteps. Not in fire, but in rhythm.

Which brings me to my friend, Drew.

If you met Drew today—passing him at the grocery store, sitting next to him at a game, or watching him walk into a room—you might not think anything was unusual about him. He doesn't carry himself like someone trying to make a scene or get attention. He isn't flashy or dramatic. He's just... consistent. Remarkably consistent.

But the truth is, Drew is one of the most transformational human beings I have ever known.

He has been called the *Energizer Bunny* —the *pulse of the room*. A nationally recognized high school teacher. A father. A husband. A mentor. A coach. A craftsman. And yet, those titles don't begin to describe the impact he has had on thousands of people.

To me, Drew is something even more rare:
A human being who does ordinary things with sacred intention.

Let me explain.

Drew did not come from wealth. His beginnings were humble. He grew up learning the value of labor—real labor. The kind that demands sweat, knees in the dirt, hands worn raw. He learned to work with tools, wood, nails, and floors. Every summer, you can find him on his hands and knees installing custom hardwood flooring in someone's house in the community. I've worked alongside him during a remodel he helped me with, and I was blown away by what I saw: every tool, every board, every movement was intentional. He didn't rush. He didn't cut corners. He didn't need supervision. His consistency was breathtaking.

And here's the thing: Drew wasn't *trying* to impress anybody.
He wasn't taking pictures.
He wasn't building a brand.
He wasn't chasing status.
He was simply honoring the ordinary with devotion.

It is almost unbelievable—especially in a world where people do things only when they feel inspired or when someone is watching. But Drew doesn't operate that way. He is the same from sunrise to sunset, in public or in private, when rewarded or when unnoticed. When Drew enters any room, he instantly becomes the hardest worker in it—not because he is competing, but because his consistency is who he is.

And yet, his consistency is not what makes him extraordinary.
It is the **intention** behind it.

Let me show you.

Drew has been a high school teacher for nearly thirty years. He did not choose teaching to gain recognition, wealth, or status. He chose it to change lives. And he has, more than he will ever know. If we do rough math—thirty years, five to six classes a year, twenty-five to thirty students per class—we're already talking about over **5,000 students.** And that number doesn't include the hundreds he coached in sports and debate, or the thousands he mentored beyond school hours.

Consistency in Drew's classroom looks like this: every class period, he stands outside his door. Rain, snow, exhaustion, good days, bad days—it doesn't matter. He is there, greeting every student by name with a handshake, a smile, and some personal line only a real relationship would allow.

EVERY. SINGLE. CLASS.

Across three decades.

Think back for a moment: how many teachers in your entire educational career greeted you at the door every day, by name, with sincerity? Most of us can't think of one; I certainly can't.

Inside the classroom, the same sacred consistency continues. Eye contact—every time a student speaks. A knee to the ground next to the desk of a student asking a serious question. Moving around the room so everyone feels seen.

Celebrating student comments with:

"Thank you for sharing." "Thank you for taking a risk." Or when someone offers an insight that goes deeper—"Wow. Goosebumps." (And he would look down at his arms as if he could see them rise.)

Simple. Ordinary. Consistent.

And because of that consistency, students open up; they take risks; they transform. Considering the competition for attention our youth face today, the focus on self-image, and the vulnerability they experience in during formative years. These simple yet consistent steps Drew takes help students feel safe to be themselves at a time when they are most afraid to open up to others.

He says things like, "Are you picking up what I'm throwing down?" or "Let me hook you up like a tow truck," and the kids smile—not because the lines are flashy, but because they are *the same lines*, day after day, year after year. The familiarity makes them feel safe. The ritual makes them feel connected. The consistency makes them feel valued.

Over time, Drew's students learn something sacred:

Showing up matters. Showing up with love matters more.

Imagine the number of lunchrooms, grocery stores, sporting events, and city corners where Drew runs into former students. I have been with him dozens of times, and it became a ritual: someone would walk up, and Drew would instantly say their name, remember their life, and treat them like a lifelong friend. I eventually stopped asking how he knew them. The answer was always the same:

"They're my buddy."

And he meant it. Truthfully, they were all former students he had—or even their parents. Drew was known amongst parents as a sought-after teacher. Families with several kids made sure each one took at least one of Drew's classes in high school. I've been at community events and professional gatherings where he inevitably became a topic of discussion because several people in the room had kids who'd been his students.

Every comment about him being one of impact on their kids and family.

Thousands of people, all convinced they are one of Drew's best friends—because he makes every person feel like they matter. Not in a grand gesture. Not in a dramatic speech.

But in ordinary, sacred consistency.

In a lineup, Drew might appear like anyone else.
But people like Drew are rare.
You can't see consistency at a glance.
You feel it over time.

Anyone can do something once.
Anyone can be passionate once.
Anyone can be inspired once.

But Drew does it every day. Every year. For decades.

This is the difference between a transformational moment and a transformational life.

Do Ordinary Things with Sacred Intention

Drew taught me something profound: **Transformation is not a moment. It is a rhythm.**

Most people chase the "big" moments—breakthroughs, achievements, new habits, new years, new goals. But the truth is, transformation rarely shows up in fireworks. Most of the time, it shows up in the *mundane*—the tiny decisions we make when no one is watching.

Anyone can be inspired once.
Anyone can change their attitude for a day.
Anyone can promise themselves improvement in January.

But the transformed? They are consistent.

Consistency is the mortar between the bricks. It is what holds purpose, commitment, language, and vulnerability together day after day on our journey. We love the idea of transformation, but we drastically underestimate the discipline of it.

Most people believe transformation happens because of a single event:

- a retreat
- a crisis
- a breakthrough
- a moment of vulnerability
- an inspiring message

And sometimes it does. But without consistency, transformation becomes a memory, not a lifestyle.

It becomes, *"There was this one time…"* rather than, *"This is who I am now."* There is so much beauty in the mundane. We tend to believe greatness is found in extraordinary acts, but in my work and research I have found something else is true: **extraordinary lives are built on ordinary days.**

Not extraordinary talent.
Not extraordinary intelligence.
Not extraordinary luck.

Ordinary days. Ordinary choices. Ordinary habits.
Done with sacred intention.

Small and simple things bring about great things. Drew never set out to become a nationally recognized teacher. He just showed up—again and again and again—with the same consistency, honor, and love. That is where the real magic lives.

The Habit of Becoming

More than 2,000 years ago, Aristotle said what every modern leadership book keeps trying to rephrase: "We are what we repeatedly do. Excellence, therefore, is not an act, but a habit."

What makes this powerful is not the poetry but the truth. You are not *what* you intend to do, or what you believe you could do, or what you did once—you are what you do *consistently*. Ask, "Who is a runner?" The answer isn't the person who ran last year; it's the one who runs regularly, every single day without question. This brings about a great point of suffering: it's not easy to run every day, just as it's not easy to stay intentionally consistent—it's difficult. Running in many respects is suffering on the body, lungs, and heart, but in a good way. Therefore, our consistency in habits will be expectedly difficult as well. Do you think it's easy for Drew to show up the same way for thirty years in the classroom? A resounding

"No." It's hard and takes purpose, commitment, and vulnerability. All of which we have hereto discussed. Yet consistency holds things together on the daily, like mortar holds bricks.

Habits reveal identity. Consistency shapes character. Rituals build culture. Drew never had to tell students what he believed about them; they felt it—every day—for years. This is how transformation moves from idea to reality: through repetition, through practice, through sacred routine.

Neuroscience confirms what Aristotle intuited: the brain is built for consistency. Repeated actions literally rewire neural pathways—habits carve them, repetition strengthens them, and intention gives them meaning. When you do something once, the brain notices; do it again, the brain prepares for it; do it repeatedly, the brain automates it. That is why habits are so powerful: they can conserve energy, reduce decision fatigue, build identity, and shape behavior without force. And when we repeat an action with intention, the brain pairs the habit with meaning—over time, the body begins to want what the heart knows is good. This is why consistency changes us, not occasionally, but fundamentally.

Of course, not all consistency is created equal. There is a rote, mechanical version that feels emotionless, and another born of fear—rigid, controlling, performative. Neither transforms; they are transactional. The consistency that transforms is the consistency of conscience: doing what is right, again and again, even when unseen, even when ignored, even when uncelebrated. Because absolute consistency is rooted in values, not visibility. Drew didn't greet students at the door for recognition; he did it for dignity. He did it because every student deserved to be seen. He did it because love—real love—is consistent. And that kind of consistency, practiced over years, becomes a legacy.

Consistency at Scale

We might ask, "This sounds great, but Drew is one person. How do groups, organizations, and communities develop this?" The answer: intentionally.

Consistency is where transformation is either won or lost. We realized this early on with our leadership programming; everything we built in Groundwork was designed around that reality: repetition.

When I first began working with leaders, I noticed something formative. People could have emotional breakthroughs—deep purpose, powerful insights, renewed commitment—but without consistent habits, nothing changed. They left inspired... and returned to life unchanged.

So, we designed Groundwork differently.

Our leadership institute was not a one-time retreat or workshop. It was a structure of consistent learning, consistent reflection, consistent community, consistent habits. We knew that if transformation was a journey, we had to build a **road**, not a **moment**.

Month after month, session after session, ritual after ritual, leaders practiced the same behaviors: they opened meetings with purpose. They created space for vulnerability. They celebrated commitments. They used shared language. They held each other accountable. And just as in Drew's classroom, something profound began to happen: **transformation became predictable.**

We could actually **anticipate** when a breakthrough was coming.

Around month two or three, leaders started seeing the world differently. Around month four or five, behaviors began to change. Around month six, transformation was no longer theory—it was life.

Not because we told them what to think, but because they started **practicing** what they believed.

Organizations are no different than people. They don't rise to the level of their mission. They fall to the level of their habits and processes. A team can have a brilliant strategy—without consistency, it dissolves into aspiration. A culture can have inspiring values—without consistency, they become posters on a wall. A company can have passionate leaders—without consistency, people return to default.

Consistency is the system that makes transformation sustainable.

It's found in the daily, weekly, and monthly practices. As the CEO of a healthcare facility, I saw that the success of our outcomes, both financially and clinically, depended on how well our daily, weekly, and monthly practices were in place. How it impacted the personal habits of my department heads. The way leaders showed up when tired, discouraged, or overwhelmed. The systems pulled us through on hard days.

Many organizations lose battles not because they lack talent or desire, but because they cannot sustain effort over time. They want transformation without repetition. They want breakthrough without discipline. They want a strong culture without consistency. But the leaders in Groundwork taught us this truth: *transformation becomes identity only when it becomes routine.*

Consistency Makes Transformation Real

In Chapter 8, we talked about vulnerability as a doorway. When opened, transformation rushes in. But a doorway is only an entry. You still must *walk* the path, and that path is paved with consistency.

Someone can have a breakthrough moment, a deep insight, a change of heart, a moment of awakening—but without consistency, the transformation fades into a distant memory. How many people do you know who have had life-changing moments, only to slowly drift back to who they were before?

Not because they were bad.
Not because they lacked wisdom.
Not because the insight wasn't real.

But because transformation requires structure.
It requires repetition.
It requires habits.

Transformation without consistency is inspiration.
Transformation with consistency becomes identity.

If you look closely at people who are transformed—not once, but continually—you notice something simple: they do not rise to the level of inspiration. They fall to the level of their habits.

In fact, most of the transformation people admire is invisible:

- getting up when the alarm rings
- choosing patience in an argument
- finishing work you don't feel like doing
- reading when scrolling is easier
- exercising when the couch feels softer
- praying when you feel nothing
- apologizing when ego wants silence
- showing up, again and again

None of these are glamorous, none ever go viral, but this is the real and daily work of transformation. Anyone can run a marathon or install a beautiful hardwood floor—once. But a person committed to transformation trains every day. Anyone can be kind, show up in a good mood, or stand at a door and authentically greet students—for a day. But a transformed person practices kindness, even when they are exhausted. Anyone can speak beautifully on a stage or say the right thing to a young, vulnerable person—one time. But a transformed person speaks with dignity even in private, day after day.

Consistency is not exciting. But consistency is where character is proven and transformative power lives.

And that is why it is sacred.

Ordinary as Sacred

In Western culture, we tend to separate the sacred from the ordinary—as if the holy exists only in places of worship or in moments of ritual, prayer, or spiritual ceremony. But ancient cultures never made that division. They believed the sacred was woven into daily life: preparing food, sweeping floors, teaching children, tending land, greeting others, and working with your hands. There was no "ordinary." There was only *intention*. Drew lives this truth without ever needing to explain it. Every handshake feels like the breath of life. Every comment and every broken-down sentence remind himself and others who they are and what their potential is. Every moment of eye contact beckoning vulnerability from others—it is ordinary, but sacred.

There is a spiritual texture to consistency. It tells the world: "I will not treat this moment casually. I will not treat this person casually. I will not treat life casually." And when you do ordinary things with sacred intention, the world responds differently. People soften. Trust deepens. Respect grows. Potential surfaces. Transformation breathes. This indeed forecasts the following two conditions of transformation: Deep and Trusting Relationships, and Safe Spaces to Learn and Practice.

And if you think ordinary doesn't matter, just **consider the math.** Thirty years. Five to six classes a year. Twenty-five to thirty students in each class. Over 5,000 students; 5,000 handshakes at the door; 5,000 "thank you for sharing;" 5,000 "I'm going to hook you up like a tow truck;" 5,000 moments of eye contact; 5,000 tiny acts of dignity. We often underestimate the compounding power of ordinary love. One handshake means little. Five thousand handshakes change a generation. One class is ordinary. Thirty years is transformational. One child having one safe adult can change their life. Imagine 5,000.

Drew will never track the numbers. He will never call himself exceptional. He will never ask to be seen. But his consistency made him a force of transformation—ordinary things, sacred intention, repeated without fanfare. **That is the recipe.**

Indigenous Wisdom on Consistency

*Mālama –
(mAH-lah-mah)*
Hawaiian, "to care
for, to preserve, to
serve, to protect."

Across Indigenous cultures, consistency is not mechanical—it is sacred. In Hawaii, the word **mālama** (*mAH-lah-mah*) means "to care for, to preserve, to serve, to protect." But mālama is not a one-time act. It is daily stewardship. Ancient Hawaiians believed the land would only care for them if they cared for it—every day. Taro fields, fishponds, irrigation lines, and crops were tended to not with convenience but with devotion. Not occasionally, but continually. Small acts. Daily care. Generational impact. This is the heart of consistency: taking care of something as if it were alive because your intention gives it life.

Your relationships need mālama.
Your leadership needs mālama.
Your transformation needs mālama.

*Pōwhiri –
(poh-fe-ree)*
Māori, "Welcome
ceremony"

*Haka –
(hah-kah)*
Māori, "Dance of
unity and strength"

Hongi –(ong-ee)
Māori, "Sacred
breath-sharing
greeting"

The **Māori** of Aotearoa understood this as well. In Māori culture, repetition is not monotony; repetition is meaning. Rituals make relationships strong and safe. The **pōwhiri** (*poh-fe-ree*), the welcoming ceremony, does not change. The **haka** (*hah-kah*), the dance of unity and strength, does not change. The **hongi** (*ong-ee*), the sacred breath-sharing greeting, does not change. Why? Because ritual creates identity. Identity creates belonging. Belonging creates strength. And strength—like love—is revealed through consistency. That is why Māori warriors used the same haka for generations, why ancestors carved the same symbols into the Marae, and why families told the same creation stories for centuries. Repetition was not boring. It was sacred. It is the same reason Drew repeats the same gestures, the same greetings, the same affirmations with every new class. He is not trying to be clever—he is trying to be constant. Because transformation is not in novelty. Transformation is in consistency.

O po –(oh-poh)
Filipino, "Phrase
conveying respect"

The **Philippines** holds this same wisdom. Filipinos have a daily linguistic ritual of "**o po**" (*oh-poh*)—a short and straightforward phrase you will hear every Filipino repeat at the end of a sentence with others, after a greeting of hello or goodbye, and in every conversation. It is a consistent filler word that conveys respect for another person. This phrase has Indigenous and sacred roots. If you read the preface, you will recall me describing the gesture in the Philippines called mano po—a simple gesture in which a younger person takes the hand of an elder and places it on their own forehead as a sign of respect and blessing.

Why?

In the islands, there is a belief in mana, or spiritual power, in all living things, and Indigenous Filipinos believed the head contained the most mana in a human being. In kind, our elders have higher mana and/or wisdom. Therefore, gently placing their hand on your forehead was believed to be a literal transfer of mana and blessing. Two seconds. One motion. Done every day. Simple. Ordinary. Consistent. Yet inside that tiny ritual lives heritage, humility, and honor. Children grow up with it. Parents expect it. Grandparents feel it. Elders pass it on. The act is small, but the meaning is enormous. This is consistency—small acts, sacred intention, generational impact. Drew's classroom rituals are just modern versions of mano po: seeing people, honoring people, blessing people, every day. And that is why transformation happens around him.

We drink from wells we did not dig. We eat fruit from trees we did not plant. We are loved because someone before us refused to stop loving. In the same way, when we are consistent in doing ordinary things with sacred intention, we become ancestors of transformation. Even if we never see the fruit. Even if those who benefit never know our names. Pamana teaches this truth: you do not plant seeds for applause. You plant them for those who will walk this earth long after you are gone.

Grit: the Strength to Stay the Course

Angela Duckworth's research on grit changed how the world understands high achievement. She defined grit as "passion and perseverance for long-term goals." Not passion alone. Not perseverance alone. Passion plus perseverance. Grit is what keeps a person consistent when motivation fades—and motivation always fades.

Passion without consistency is enthusiasm.
Consistency without passion is exhaustion.
Grit is the marriage of both.

Duckworth's findings also revealed something counterintuitive: grit predicts success more than talent, intelligence, or opportunity. Why? Because grit turns intention into reality. It turns potential into progress. It turns transformation into a lifestyle. Drew is not transformational because he is gifted. He is transformational because he is gritty.

Thirty years.
Classroom after classroom.
Handshakes.
Eye contact.
Encouragement.
Presence.

What most people would find repetitive or tiring, he treats as a privilege. His grit is not loud—it is steady. And steady changes lives.

I have learned the same lesson in my own life. I am not great at most things, but I try to be perfect at one thing—my morning ritual. For years now, every single morning—before the world wakes up—I study scripture, pray, journal, and exercise. It is not dramatic. It is not glamorous. It is not always easy. But it is sacred. It is my ritual of intention. I do it when I am tired, when I am discouraged, when nobody will ever know whether I did it or not.

I learned that I can **never miss a day,** not because I am perfect, but because I know what happens when I stop. My mind drifts. My spirit dulls. My purpose blurs. Consistency keeps me aligned. It keeps me becoming. It reminds me who I am, what I believe, and what I am called to do. On hard days when I'm tired, when I'm depressed, or even sick, the words "never miss a day" play over and over in my mind until I get myself out of bed and start making the simple and ordinary a part of living a devoted and sacred life.

And when I think about *Pamana*—legacy—I realize I am not doing these things only for myself. I am doing them for my wife, my children, the people I serve, and even those I will never meet. Just as I drink from wells I did not dig, I want to build wells for those who will live long after I am gone. Small and simple things, repeated with sacred intention, are how transformation becomes identity.

Here is the truth: *when we trust ourselves with the little things, we create a life where people trust us with the big things.*

Our consistency builds trust, period. As a leader, nothing builds trust faster—or deeper—than consistency. If people always know which version of you will walk through the door, they don't have to waste emotional energy preparing for impact. But when your presence is unpredictable—kind one day, harsh the next; engaged one week, absent the next; inspired today, exhausted tomorrow—people protect themselves.

Drew is transformational because people know exactly who he will be every time he shows up. They never wonder which version of him will arrive. He is whole, steady, present, and real. Consistency is a form of love. It tells people: "You are safe here." And when people feel safe, they open up. When they open up, they take risks. When they take risks, they grow. And when they grow, transformation happens.

Practical Framework: Ordinary with Intention

If consistency feels overwhelming, good. It means you are human. But here's the truth: consistency is not about doing everything. It's about choosing something—small, simple, sacred—and doing it every day.

Here are practical commitments to build consistency into your life:

1. Choose One Daily Habit

Not ten. Not five. One.

- Ten minutes of reading
- Thirty minutes of exercise

- Five minutes of prayer or meditation
- Sending one text of gratitude
- Taking your kids outside after work
- Eating dinner without phones

Transformation is not built in the grand. It is built in the repeatable.

2.   Make It Visible

Write it down. Put it on a calendar. Track it. Humans grow what they measure.

3.   Name Your Why

If you forget *why* you are doing something, you will stop doing it.

4.   Honor Ritual

Turn routines into meaning: light a candle before journaling. Remove shoes before prayer. Play the same song every morning. Sit in the same chair to read. *Ritual turns ordinary into sacred.*

5.   Forgive Imperfection

Missing one day is normal. Missing two days is human. Missing three days is not failure, as long as you begin again.

Consistency is not perfection. Consistency is return.

Reflection

Before you move to the next chapter, take a moment to write:

What is one ordinary habit you can practice with sacred intention every day?

____

____

What relationship needs consistency from you—not in words, but in presence?

____

____

____

Who in your life needs to know they can count on you?

____

____

____

What ritual could you create to remind you of your purpose and keep you on the path of transformation?

____

____

____

Because transformation is not an event. Transformation is a lifestyle.
Not in the dramatic. Not in the miraculous. Not in the exceptional.
But in the ordinary. Done with sacred intention.

Again and again. And again.

Commitment
Safe Space
Common Language
Purpose
Trusting Relationships
Vulnerability
Consistency

Chapter *Ten:*
GO DEEP, NOT WIDE— BUILD SOMETHING THAT WITHSTANDS THE STORMS

In a world obsessed with expansion—more followers, more contacts, more reach—*depth* has become a lost art. We build networks instead of relationships, audiences instead of communities, influence instead of *trust*.

But when the storms come—and they always come—it's not the width of our network that holds us; it's the depth and trust in our relationships. Depth withstands. Depth heals. Depth transforms.

The Power of Depth

My friend, Brian, is a profound example of what "deep" truly means in a relationship.

Years ago, when I was working as an account executive for a training and consulting firm, I saw two names appear on a client roster: Brian and Jason, real-estate developers from Salem, Oregon. They had signed up for one of our workshops on their own accord. I decided to take a chance and reached out to meet them for lunch when they came to town.

That lunch was a pivotal moment in my life.

From the first moment, Brian's presence was disarming. His questions weren't the casual kind most people ask just to be polite. He asked as though the answer mattered—as though *I* mattered. His eye contact was steady but soft, his listening full of space. I remember thinking, *no one can be this authentic all the time.* But years later, he still is.

Our first long phone conversation revealed the depth of who he was. My intent was to learn about his and Jason's vision to transform their community. What I didn't expect was that Brian would spend most of the call asking about me—my story, my hopes, my beliefs. He cultivated a depth of connection that stripped away the transactional tone of our roles. It was as if he built a bridge of trust before either of us realized it. You may know people like this—conversations with them stand out from all the others.

That single call set in motion a relationship that would change the trajectory of my life.

When Jason later offered me the opportunity that led to the creation of the leadership institute (Groundwork) and all this research, it was Brian who had already made me believe transformation was possible. Through only a handful of conversations—conversations held with such depth it felt as though he and I had known each other for a lifetime.

Over the years, I've watched Brian live the same way with everyone. In meetings as a CEO of his company, Neighborly Ventures, in breakfasts as friends, or in gatherings with hundreds of employees, he treats each conversation as if it were sacred. As if the person in front of him is the only one in existence.

Once, I invited him to speak to a cohort of leaders in Groundwork. He greeted participants by name and referenced small details about their lives. Later, several of them asked me, "How did he know those things? How did he know my name?"

I realized he had memorized their bios and faces we sent him weeks before—something all guest speakers received, but none used this way. He learned their names and details not for performance, but *for relationship*. That's Brian. He does his homework on people, not to impress them, but because he wants to *see* them.

Depth is not drama.
Depth is discipline.
And Brian lives that discipline daily.

As a business leader, a board member of a large nonprofit, and a regional religious leader, you would think the only way he could survive would be to treat interactions transactionally—surface-deep. That is what many high-capacity leaders do because their bandwidth is so limited. But Brian is the opposite. I once sat in a meeting with his executive team where I was presenting the results of an organizational assessment. Some results were not favorable. Instead of becoming defensive, I saw in his eyes a genuine eagerness to learn and make things right for his people.

In that same meeting, he said, "If we aren't running a company where people are seen and relationships are valued, then I don't want to be the CEO. We might do real estate, but what matters most is that our one hundred-plus employees feel like they matter." Again, this is a nice thought of a gesture I have heard other CEOs say, but few ever follow through on it. He did. At his next all-company meeting, he publicly apologized to his employees for his leadership failures.

Vulnerable, yes. Risky, no. Because of the authenticity he had shown up with day in and day out before that moment.

Truth be told, what I learned in the assessment was that *every* employee felt deeply seen and cared for by Brian. They felt the depth of his care in every interaction. The issues were with other leaders in the company. Unknowingly, Brian had set such a high standard for relational depth and trust by simply being himself that it was difficult for others to match. A good problem to have, by the way, because I've seen the opposite far too often: leaders who evoke anxiety and perfection rather than genuine trust and depth.

The irony in Brian's interactions is that he does not project perfection. He openly admits his faults, his struggles, and his imperfections, which, as I have seen time and time again, is one of the most powerful ways to build trust.

While Brian carries influence across multiple spheres, he treats every relationship with depth and purpose. And as a result—speaking for myself and many others—there is no storm our relationship cannot withstand.

Trust as the Outcome

If Brian taught me depth, Salam taught me trust.

If you asked anyone in Salem to list the most influential people in the community, Salam's name would likely be near the top. Not because he seeks attention—he doesn't. Not because he collects credit—he rarely accepts any. His influence runs deep precisely *because* it is built on trust.

Salam is old enough to be my father, yet he treats me like an equal. The same man who once served as Oregon's director of education—who earned the highest degrees in his discipline, who carries decades of impact—now spends his days mentoring leaders across sectors: education, nonprofit, government, business, and faith. He is the kind of leader who could command any room, but instead, he empowers others to lead. Over and over again, we've found ourselves in rooms where he could easily take the reins, yet he handed them to me. Each time, he deepened our trust. And each time, I trusted him more.

He was there in that sacred moment years ago when we shared the Unggno—the breath of life—with fifteen community leaders. That moment helped spark the early realization of what would later become Culture of One. Since then, Salam has become both a mentor and a brother to me. He has been a steady force in my life—quiet, powerful, and unwavering.

His superpower is simple but rare:
he builds trust so deep it transforms systems.

One of the clearest examples happened within the Salem school district—one of the largest in Oregon. Two high schools were among the lowest-performing in the state. Salam, already retired, volunteered to help. The goal was ambitious: increase graduation rates by 10 percentage points in four years.

They did it in one.

And they didn't do it through new policies, expensive technologies, or flashy initiatives. They did it through trust.

The students most at risk of dropping out—called "bubble students"—were each paired with an advocate: a teacher, coach, or counselor who committed not just to monitoring them, but walking with them. Truly *walking* with them. I sat in rooms with these advocates and these students. I listened to their stories. I witnessed their love and trust for one another. What began as surface-level support became the kind of relationship that changes the trajectory of a young person's life.

Salam modeled this for the school leadership teams. He made trust feel both safe and required. Leaders began trusting their staff more deeply. Staff trusted the advocates. And the advocates trusted the students enough to stay with them through every late assignment, every setback, every moment of doubt.

The result? Out of forty-nine bubble seniors, forty-seven graduated.

Not because of new programs.
Not because of new funding.
Because someone believed in them.
Because trust created possibility.
Because depth created safety.

Trust changed the data.

Don't get me wrong. There was funding, there were systems built, there were strategies deployed, but the difference at the end of the day that cannot be easily replicated was the level of depth and trust in the relationships. I have found that nothing moves the needle faster and more sustainably than trust. The challenge, as we will explore in this chapter, is that *trust is an outcome, not a prerequisite.*

True to form, Salam never asked for recognition. He didn't want a headline or a plaque. He simply knew—deep in his bones—that when trust is built, transformation follows. That's the quiet power of depth. That's

Salam's gift. And that is why so many people, myself included, would follow him anywhere.

What the Research Says

Our institute's research confirmed what we witnessed: transformation thrives where trust runs deep. Every year, we analyzed our programs—collecting data —and one finding stood above the rest: the most transformative experiences came from *deep, trusting relationships*. The most discussed theme in our research, after Vulnerability, was Deep and Trusting Relationships. It was so viscerally memorable, it was tangible. Leaders and participants could point to it, measure it, and talk about it in such a way that it became clear it was not only an outcome of the conditions that came before it, but it was a key milestone on the journey of transformation.

We found leaders who engaged in both **mentoring** and **community digs**—our designed trust-building practices—showed the highest growth in self-reported transformation scores.

This is consistent with decades of research across psychology, education, and organizational science:

- **Harvard's eighty-year study of adult development** found that the single greatest predictor of lifelong health and happiness is *the quality of relationships*—not career success, wealth, or fame.

- **Brené Brown's research** on vulnerability shows that trust is built in small moments of reliability and empathy, not grand gestures.

- **Stephen Covey** called trust "the one thing that changes everything." In organizations, high-trust cultures report higher engagement, faster decision-making, and greater innovation.

- **John Gottman's relationship studies** show that trust grows when positive interactions outnumber negative ones at least five to one—a ratio that applies as much in boardrooms as in marriages.

Trust and depth are not soft skills; they are survival skills. And like any skill, they can be practiced and strengthened. Brian and Salam did not suddenly arrive at this ability to build such strong relationships; it came from years of work within themselves to authentically show up for others when in a relationship. Just as I have shared with Indigenous beliefs about this "space between"—concepts like Vā and Kapwa— they highlight the value and importance of the relationship over self. More important than the self or the other—you and me—is the space between us—the relationship. This is what matters. This is what needs healing when things go wrong. This is what makes the difference when things go right. The space between us and others is not a philosophical concept; it is life. We live, so do others, and our connection to each other is living to. If that connection dies, so do we.

That is why our ancestors referred to this connection as the most sacred.

The Indigenous Lens: Relationship as Sacred

In Indigenous worldviews across the Asia-Pacific, it is understood that relationships are not transactional—they are sacred. The Māori word **whanaungatanga** (*fah-nah-oo-nga-tah-nga*) means "kinship, relationship, and shared experience." It speaks to the deep responsibility people have to one another within a tribe or community. In Filipino culture, bayanihan means "to carry together," capturing the spirit of communal help that binds people through shared trust.

Whanaungatanga – (fah-nah-oo-nga-tah-nga) Māori, "Kinship, relationship, and shared experience"

In these traditions, relationships are not built for utility. They are built for continuity. They are not for performance but for presence. They relied on them not only for physical and literal survival, but for emotional and spiritual meaning.

When elders pass on wisdom, they don't lecture—they share stories. When communities make decisions, they don't rush—they listen. Every exchange reinforces belonging.

And belonging, as modern neuroscience now proves, is not a luxury—it's oxygen.

Relationships are the nervous system of transformation.
Without them, every other condition collapses.

Deep and Trusting Relationships in Practice

In our leadership institute, *Deep and Trusting Relationships* became the beating heart of every cohort. We built it intentionally, not incidentally.

MENTORING

Each cohort was paired with mentors—alumni from previous years. These inter-cohort bonds extended transformation beyond the classroom. Our data showed that those who actively engaged in mentoring—whether as mentor or mentee—reported far greater growth. Mentorship created generational wisdom within the program itself, the same way Pamana carries legacy across time.

COMMUNITY DIGS

Then came the "community digs." Small groups of three to four leaders were assigned to meet between sessions, with one purpose: *go deep*. Not to discuss projects or share resumes—but to know each other's stories. They later presented their discoveries creatively to the whole cohort. What began as an "icebreaker" evolved into sacred space.

Leaders cried. They forgave.
They laughed. They listened.

One leader said, "I trust some of you more than the people I live with every day." And we knew then: transformation was happening. Not in theory. In relationship.

Depth is Built, Not Found

We often confuse *trust* with *agreeance* and *depth* with *understanding*. But trust isn't about always seeing eye to eye; it's about always seeing heart to heart. Depth doesn't require sameness; it requires commitment.

Deep and trusting relationships grow through:

- **Purpose:** Shared meaning gives direction to connection.
- **Commitment:** Showing up even when it's inconvenient.
- **Common Language:** Words that align, not divide.
- **Vulnerability:** Willingness to be seen without armor.
- **Consistency:** Reliability that earns respect.

Each of the previous conditions makes this one possible. Together, they form the foundation that allows relationships to move beyond convenience—to become covenant.

As my friend, Chad Ford, writes in *Dangerous Love*, "When we choose to see people as people, not objects, we open the possibility for peace." That is agape—the unconditional love that makes depth possible.

When that level of trust is reached, it becomes nearly unbreakable. No disagreement can fracture it. No storm can wash it away.

I have seen leaders in our cohorts who, before participating in our institute, attempted to sabotage each other, only to go on to build a relationship so deep that I witnessed them seeking forgiveness with tears streaming down their faces in quiet rooms. I have seen elected leaders on different sides of the political aisle who would have never connected privately, form bonds that now have them meeting regularly for lunch. I have seen other leaders who knew nothing about the others in the room end up regularly connecting not only to address community challenges, but also to fortify their relationships, for the sake of the relationship itself—not for a self-serving benefit.

Here is the thing about a relationship with the depth and trust that can withstand a storm. They are perpetual. They are sustainable.

What we are talking about here is not acquaintanceship. We're not talking about casual relationships built on politeness, agreement, or convenience. We're talking about **deep and trusting relationships**—the kind that cannot be shaken by disagreement, distance, or difficulty. These kinds of relationships take time, intention, courage, and effort.

While Kapwa and Vā remind us that we are always in relation to one another, the choice to go *deep* is another level entirely. Anyone can share space; very few choose to share themselves. Trust, at this level, is not an event but a slow and intentional layering—built in moments of vulnerability, reinforced in moments of consistency, strengthened in moments of choice. The more we invest, the deeper it becomes. The deeper it becomes, the more unbreakable it gets. Brian and Salam embody this. Both men model what it looks like to show up with courage, curiosity, and presence every single time. They remind us that depth is not accidental—it is cultivated. Their relationships with me and countless others were not built in a day; they were built in hundreds of small moments when they chose depth over transaction.

And the truth is, there is no ceiling to that depth. There is no limit to the trust two people can build when they keep showing up for each other. Or what an organization, or even a community, can accomplish with deep and trusting relationships. When this kind of relationship forms, you reach a point where there is almost nothing the other person could do that would undo that bond. Love is in the equation—not romantic love, but the kind of unconditional regard that sees the whole human and stays.

At this level, trust no longer depends on agreement. You don't have to see issues the same way to stand with each other. You don't have to understand someone fully to believe in them. This kind of trust fortifies the space between people like Kevlar—resilient, protective, and nearly indestructible. Salam proved this in the schools he supported, where deep trust between adults and students produced outcomes that data alone could never achieve. Brian proved it in his companies, where people performed—not because they feared him, but because they trusted him. Depth became their infrastructure.

This level of relationship isn't just personally transformative—it is organizationally catalytic. Teams that intentionally cultivate deep and trusting relationships don't crumble under pressure; they become stronger. When conflict arises, they move toward each other instead of away. When stress increases, they collaborate instead of compete. Innovation flows more freely because safety is high. Accountability is real because people feel responsible for one another, not just for their own work. People stop being "held accountable;" rather, accountable people are created. Organizations that go deep—where leaders know their people, understand their stories, and value their humanity—outperform those that merely go wide. In-kind relationships at home and elsewhere that focus on depth rather than breadth become unbreakable. Disagreements, mistakes, and even intentionally harmful words can be worked through. Not easy—but more possible when the depth of the relationship has been the priority. Wide will get you visibility and attention. Deep will get you resilience and longevity.

This is why "go deep, not wide" is more than a catchy saying—it is a condition for transformation. Wide relationships help you grow a network. Deep relationships help you build a life. Wide gives you reach. Deep gives you roots. Wide is how you expand. Deep is how you survive. And in a world obsessed with more—more followers, more teams, more initiatives, more everything—depth is the countercultural choice that actually withstands the storms.

What Depth Looks Like

Depth is not always dramatic. It's often found in the smallest gestures:

- Sitting with your child for five minutes to just listen.
- A colleague understanding their impact on others who then does something intentional to strengthen that relationship.
- Sending a message that says, "I thought of you today," without expecting a reply.
- Asking, "What's really going on?"—and staying quiet long enough to hear the truth.

Trust is built in moments like these. Over time, they accumulate into something immovable.

What matters is not any single gesture, but what those gestures signal when they are repeated: *you matter here; I am paying attention; this space is safe enough to stay.* These moments rarely announce themselves as transformational. They often feel ordinary, even forgettable. And yet, they quietly do the work that strategies, policies, and declarations cannot.

This is where transformation begins to take shape between people.

Not because one condition is executed perfectly, but because several are lived consistently. Purpose gives meaning to why we show up. Commitment keeps us showing up when it's inconvenient. Language helps us understand one another. Vulnerability allows truth to surface. Consistency turns isolated moments into a pattern. When these conditions intersect, something new forms—not by force, but by design.

That *something* is depth. And depth, over time, becomes trust.

What follows is not accidental. It is sequential.

The Sequence of Transformation

In the journey of the 7 Conditions, **Deep and Trusting Relationships** emerge as the natural outcome of the earlier ones—and the necessary foundation for what follows.

- **Purpose** anchors relationships in meaning.
- **Commitment** keeps us showing up.
- **Common Language** lets us be understood.
- **Vulnerability** opens the door to truth.
- **Consistency** turns moments into habits.
- **Deep and Trusting Relationships** form when all of these meet in the space between people.

And those relationships, in turn, create the final condition—**Safe Space to Learn and Practice**—where transformation becomes sustainable.

Trust is both the bridge and the shelter. It connects and protects. It gives depth to what we do at home and at work.

When trust is present, people stop performing and start participating. They risk honesty. They admit what they don't know. They try, fail, learn, and try again without fear of being discarded. Growth accelerates not because expectations disappear, but because safety allows truth to surface and mistakes to become teachers instead of threats.

This is why trust is not a "soft" outcome of transformation—it is a structural necessity. Without it, learning becomes dangerous, vulnerability becomes costly, and change collapses under the weight of fear. With it, people stretch, experiment, and evolve together. What began as individual choices becomes a shared environment—one capable of holding transformation over time.

And that environment is where we turn next.

Reflection

Take time this week to reflect and act:

Who are the few people in your life or work who have earned your deepest trust? What made it possible?

____

____

____

Where are you spreading yourself too thin—staying wide instead of deep?

____

____

____

Who have you been distant from but know deserves another chance?

____

____

____

What relationships in your leadership, family, or community would transform if you gave them time, vulnerability, and consistency?

____

____

____

Practice

- **Choose one person** to go deeper with this week. Schedule time with them that has no agenda—just curiosity.

- **Listen longer than you speak.** Pay attention to what is not said.

- **End your next meeting with gratitude.** Name something you admire in the person or group.

- **Keep a "trust journal."** Write one example each day of someone showing up for you—or you showing up for them.

Depth is not built in days; it's built over time. So start small. Be consistent. Go deep, not wide. Build something that will withstand the storms.

Commitment
Safe Space
Common Language
Purpose
Trusting Relationships
Vulnerability
Consistency

Chapter *Eleven:*
CREATE SPACE FOR BECOMING

Becoming. It's a word we've touched on repeatedly throughout this book, and for good reason. Becoming is not achievement. It is not perfection. It is not a destination or a title. Becoming is the movement of a life toward its potential—sometimes slow, sometimes sudden, often painful, always intentional. Becoming is transformation in motion. It is the trajectory of identity reshaping itself through choice, discomfort, and possibility.

This seventh condition—Safe Space—is the capstone of the entire journey. It is where all previous conditions converge and where the next iteration of transformation prepares to unfold. In the research, this condition emerged under the theme, "Safe Space to Learn, Practice, and Fail," but that phrase is too long for everyday use. Instead, we call it Safe Space. Not the modern trendy version of emotional bubble wrap or psychological insulation. This is not a space free from difficulty. In fact, true safe space, as I found in my research, is paradoxical: it contains danger. It requires risk. It demands discomfort. It is the only soil where becoming can grow.

Transaction is the opposite of becoming. Transaction keeps us safe, predictable, guarded, and small. Becoming requires vulnerability, purpose, commitment, common language, consistency, and deep relationships—every preceding condition. Safe Space is where those conditions breathe into life. It is where we step into the unknown so that transformation can take shape.

Nowhere is this truth clearer than in the story of my dear friend, Colby.

Break Open, Don't Break

"I am taking my mother to the shelter tomorrow, and I don't know if I'll see her again."

Those were the words running through Colby's mind the day before everything broke open. He sat alone in a familiar parking lot—a place he had often gone to find peace, a place where he could breathe, think, and speak honestly with God. That day, the parking lot became its own kind of sanctuary—a small, sacred safe space where he could wrestle with the unbearable.

His mother—brilliant, creative, once full of life—had been consumed by addiction for years. She had cycled through eight rehabilitation programs, spent time homeless, and drifted through the streets in ways no son should ever have to witness. Every relapse rewrote the story he prayed would end differently. Every phone call carried the fear that this might be the last time. He loved her deeply. And yet he felt powerless. He believed, for years, that he could not help her. That her pain was beyond him. That addiction had claimed too much.

That morning, grief sat heavy in his chest. The kind that makes breathing feel complicated. He bowed his head and prayed—not the controlled, composed kind, but the kind that sounds more like a plea—a desperate conversation.

God, show me what to do. Show me what I cannot see.

What he received wasn't an answer. It was a question. A whisper of truth that felt both familiar and terrifying:

"How can you use your talents and abilities to help her? What if you could create a space where she could become again?"

He resisted at first. *Who am I to do that? What do I know about addiction? What can I offer that eight rehabilitation centers could not?* But the question wouldn't leave. It sat with him. Pressed into him. Opened something in him.

He began to think about the things that had once made his mother feel alive—her creativity, her art, her love of story, painting, color, and imagination—combined with his love for entrepreneurship and creation. Possibility flickered.

And the next morning, instead of walking his mother back into a shelter, he walked her into his home.

He wasn't rescuing her.
He wasn't fixing her.
He wasn't forcing her.

He was **creating a space** where something could happen—something sacred, something human, something transformational. Because what we've learned again and again is this:

Transformation is caught, not taught.
It is discovered, not delivered.
It is uncovered, not imposed.

At his kitchen table, they began writing a children's book—something she had always dreamed of doing but had never believed she could complete. And so they wrote. They painted. They crafted. They created.

What Colby didn't realize at the time was that he was doing the deepest work a person can do for another. He created a space where she could rediscover her purpose, her identity, her dignity, her creativity, her self-worth.

He created a space where she could **become** again.

With the person who once gave him birth and his initial breath of life. He was, in turn, helping her discover a rebirth of who she was by sharing the breath of life with her.

A space where her pain no longer disqualified her—it informed her. A space where her failures were not evidence of worthlessness—but worthiness to the story she was meant to tell. A space where her Pamana, her past, could be redeemed as wisdom for the future. A space where presence—Unggno—breathed life back into her. A space where Kapwa—the connection between them, mother and her child —carried them forward.

This is the difference between breaking apart and breaking open.
Breaking apart pushes us deeper into despair.
Breaking open reveals what is still alive in us.

And it worked.

Not instantly.
Not magically.
Not without setbacks.

But it worked.

Today, years later, she is sober.
She is creating.
She is thriving.
She is generous with her gifts.
She is alive in ways no traditional program ever unlocked.

All because Colby helped create **space**—the kind of space where becoming is possible.

But this moment didn't appear out of nowhere. It was the culmination of a life preparing him—quietly, painfully, beautifully—for this very moment.

Long Before He Knew, He Knew

Colby grew up inside a tension that would shape his entire worldview—a life filled with joy and instability, success and collapse, potential and pain. His mother battled addiction. His father—disciplined, talented, determined—tried to hold the family together until the pressure eventually broke him too. Colby watched the two people who gave him life fall from heights he once admired.

He watched them break.
He watched them lose everything.
But he has also watched them rebuild.

Pain was not a concept for him. It was a classroom. So was resilience.

Life had been teaching him—long before research, counseling, or reflection ever named it—that becoming happens in places where: failure is allowed, feedback is welcomed, discomfort is expected, refinement is constant, small things matter, and identity is formed, not performed.

He learned first through action sports in his youth that failure is necessary. Individual sports are games played against yourself, requiring discipline and consistency over and over again. Skateboarding, specifically, wasn't just a hobby for him; it became a philosophy. When a skateboarder falls, they don't interpret it as failing—they interpret it as information. **Falling is feedback**. Every bruise is a lesson. Every missed trick is a micro-adjustment. Every repetition is a refinement. Over time, micro-adjustments become instinct. Instinct becomes identity. Identity becomes confidence. Confidence becomes capacity. Through the encouragement of his father, he learned such valuable lessons as a kid, not knowing then that one day he would need to be that very encouragement for his father as he would fall, in even more devastating ways.

This is safe space.
Not a space without falling—but a space where falling is expected, observed, integrated, and redeemed.

Then he learned it again through team sports, where he and I actually met as collegiate soccer players and teammates. What struck me most was his ability to hold two truths simultaneously: he was the most talented player on the field and the most approachable person off it. He laughed easily but held high standards. He was warm and welcoming, yet fierce and demanding. He could call you out in one moment and encourage you in the next. He raised the bar without shaming anyone beneath it.

I remember a moment distinctly where, in a drill that had become tiring and repetitious, my effort and attitude began to give way—but Colby was quickly there to remind me that that was not okay. "Step it up, Pineda!" He yelled, "We need your best!" Yet I have memories of sitting in rooms with him, where his smile and welcoming demeanor made it possible for me not only to be comfortable, but also to further improve myself as an athlete and man.

That was Colby.

Direct, but caring.
Demanding, but encouraging.
Stretching you but holding you.

He created a space where people became better simply by being near him.

I have memories of sitting with him years later in a hotel room, both of us attending a professional combine. He received professional offers to play soccer—real, legitimate opportunities—but realized on that very trip something else was calling him. Purpose was calling him. Thread—a business he would later build with his wife —was calling him. Thread would eventually grow into a multi-million-dollar company, not because he chased performance, but because he cultivated becoming. He was teaching me how to let your purpose and desire *to become*, dictate the decisions you make in life.

But even Colby eventually faced his own breaking point.

Both parents collapsing at once—mother on the streets, father in prison—took a toll that no amount of grit could mask. His body shut down. Panic attacks surged. His brain locked up. He sought professional help, learned about his anxiety, and rebuilt himself using the same tools he learned as a child:

Observe. Adjust. Breathe. Refine.

One day, he told me something I have never forgotten:

"My rock bottom will always be shallow. Because I refuse to sink where I cannot climb out."

His mother taught him that.
His father taught him that.
Life taught him that.

And so he lives it.
And so he teaches it.
And so he builds spaces where others can live it too.

Because this is what safe space is:

Not the absence of pain —but the presence of possibility.
Not shelter from the storm —but strength within it.
Not protection from failure —but meaning through it.

Safe Space is the Soil of Becoming

Colby has now built two remarkable organizations: Thread and the Carry On Foundation. Both are wildly successful—not primarily because of their products or strategies, but because they were intentionally designed as environments where people can become the best versions of themselves, and those people make them successful. Yet if you ask him, his most notable achievement is his beautiful family, formed on the same foundation as everything else in his life.

Business, to Colby, is not about profit.
Sports is not about performance.
Leadership is not about authority.
Family is not about harmony.

All of them are vehicles for becoming.

And becoming requires space, space that is: safe enough to fail, structured enough to learn, challenging enough to stretch, supportive enough to rebuild, honest enough to transform, and human enough to breathe.

A safe space is not comfort—it is cultivation.

It is not a cushion—it is a container.
It is not a hiding place—it is a growing place.
It is not soft—it is sacred.

And it is always intentional.

He understands that balance is not static; rather, it is dynamic. Colby would say it's like skateboarding: the board requires constant micro-adjustments depending on the environment, angle, slope, speed, etc. Balance is not achieved once; it's practiced always. If you are on the board, balance is a constant priority.

This is why he dreams of creating the Carry-On Institute—a place where coaches, teachers, parents, and mentors can learn how to create spaces of becoming for others. Spaces where the lessons of action sports, faith, family, entrepreneurship, resilience, and purpose merge into a kind of modern Indigenous wisdom:

Observe. Adjust. Refine. Become.

He wants to create what he has already lived, because he knows what happens when someone believes in you. He knows what happens when falling becomes feedback instead of shame. He knows what happens when space is created instead of control.

He knows what happens when a mother breaks open instead of breaking apart.

And he knows that none of this is accidental. It is the final condition—the culmination of the first six. It is the container in which all other conditions breathe.

Safe Space is where transformation becomes lived. Safe Space is where becoming begins. Safe Space is where Pamana, Unggno, and Kapwa converge into the possibility of Culture of One.

Indigenous Wisdom: the Sacred Space Between

The Samoan concept of Vā, as we have discussed in other chapters, is the sacred, relational space between people. Vā is not empty. Vā is not void. Vā is alive. It is something to be protected, nurtured, and tended. When the Vā is healthy, people flourish. When the Vā is neglected, relationships fracture.

Safe Space is the Vā in action.

When Colby created space for his mother at his kitchen table, he wasn't offering physical shelter. He was tending the Vā. He was honoring the place between them—the space where her identity could heal, where her creativity could emerge, where her dignity could be restored. In Indigenous Filipino psychology, this space is also where **loob** (*lo-ob*), essentially meaning the "inner self," opens and **kalooban** (kah-loo-bahn), the "inner will," begins to strengthen again. The space is where a person remembers who they are.

Loob – (lo-ob) Filipino, "Inner self"

Kalooban – (kah-loo-bahn) Filipino, "Inner will"

Filipino psychology calls this Kapwa—shared identity, the truth that "I am who I am because of who we are." Unggno calls this breath-to-breath presence—showing up fully, without distraction. **Alaga** (*ah-lah-gah*) or "nurturing care," describes the gentle, firm attention we give in these moments—care that strengthens rather than shelters. **Hilot** (*hee-loht*), an "Indigenous healing practice," reminds us that restoration happens through presence, attunement, and balance—not force. **Pagtambayayong** (*pahg-tahm-bah-yah-yong*), a "mutual uplifting," teaches that no one becomes alone; we rise because someone rises with us.

Alaga – (ah-lah-gah) Filipino, "Nurturing care"

Hilot – (hee-loht) Filipino, "Indigenous healing practice"

Pagtambayayong – (pahg-tahm-bah-ya-yong) Filipino, "Mutual uplifting"

All of these converge in the condition of Safe Space, teaching us again that Indigenous wisdom has helped people on their journey of transformation for thousands of years.

Transformational spaces are not neutral.
They are cultivated.
They are intentional.
They are relational.
They are moral.
They are spiritual.
They require tending.

They require micro-adjustments, like the balance Colby learned in action sports—constant attunement, constant refinement.

They require courage to let another person unfold in their own timing.

Papgpapakataio (pahg-pah-pah-kah-TAH-oh) Filipino, "Becoming fully human"

They require the humility to realize we are not "fixing" someone—we are creating the environment where their **pagpapakatao** (*pahg-pah-pah-kah-TAH-oh*), the Filipino process of becoming fully human, can emerge.

This is the soil where becoming grows. This is the fruit of a well-tended relationship.

We All Seek These "Spaces"

I have another friend, Tay, whom I have known for years. From the moment I met him, I have seen his ability to create the space between him and others, one of safety. This has served him well as a cinematographer. On set, I have witnessed him help those he films—in interviews and more—feel comfortable expressing themselves, not needing to say things perfectly and allowing themselves to be vulnerable. Tay intuitively tends this space between. He softens the space without weakening it. He creates alaga—nurturing care that makes people braver, not smaller.

I have worked with him on several projects and have been amazed that the way he creates this safety mirrors what he has done for me over the years.

Tay and I have connected and collaborated on everything under the sun for over a decade now. What started out as a form of "Bible study" has morphed into constant discussion of family, business, and life. Always pushing each other. Always leaning in. Always observing, never merely seeing—because true becoming requires presence, not passivity.

It hit me recently: the reason why I enjoy him in my life is not because we share the same hobbies (we don't, for the most part). It's not because we have similar lives (we don't... at all). It is because we have formed a relationship where the space between us is sacred. Like Kapwa, we realized that *we are who we are in relation to*. We created a space between us of becoming.

And that is the essence of Safe Space. Not comfort. Not ease. Not avoidance of struggle.

But a relational field—an Indigenous Vā, a Filipino Kapwa, an Unggno breath-to-breath presence—where a person can fail safely, learn deeply, and rise again and again until they rediscover the truth of who they are becoming.

Another friend, Kasha, is also a powerful example of someone who naturally creates a Safe Space. We met in college in a facilitation course—a class designed to teach us how to guide groups, hold conversation, and create environments where learning could happen. Even then, she stood out.

She didn't stand out because she knew the most. She stood out because people felt the most human around her.

At the time, I couldn't articulate why I kept pulling her into everything—projects, events, initiatives—and later into three separate workplaces: the consulting firm where I began my career, the philanthropist's organization where my life changed, and eventually into Groundwork itself. I used to joke that she "followed me," but the truth is the opposite. I followed her. I brought her in everywhere I went—not as a favor, but out of necessity.

Only recently did I fully understand why.

Kasha makes people better. She makes rooms better. She makes *me* better.

She creates an environment—sometimes with just a glance, a joke, a nod, or the way she sits forward in a chair—where people breathe differently. Their shoulders drop. Their voices steady. Their self-doubt loosens. She brings what research calls *psychological safety* and what Indigenous wisdom calls Kapwa and Vā. She helps people become—not by teaching them something new, but by creating space where what is already inside them can rise to the surface.

Amy Edmondson's groundbreaking research on psychological safety confirms what Kasha has lived intuitively for decades: high-performing teams are not the ones with the fewest mistakes—they are the ones where people feel safe enough to admit mistakes. In environments with true psychological safety, curiosity expands, relatability increases, risk-taking becomes intelligent, people listen more deeply, learning accelerates, and honest feedback becomes normal, not threatening.

Neurobiology reinforces this. When the nervous system feels safe, the prefrontal cortex—the part of the brain responsible for insight, empathy, and problem-solving—comes online. When the nervous system feels threatened, our minds go into fight, flight, or freeze. Learning shuts down. Growth shuts down. Becoming shuts down.

But there is something Edmondson's work only hints at—something the 7 Conditions made unmistakably clear:

Safety without challenge produces stagnation.
Challenge without safety produces trauma.
The two together produce transformation.

Safe Space is not about comfort. It is about *capacity*—the capacity to stretch without snapping, to risk without collapsing, to try without pretending.

This is where Kasha, without ever naming it, embodies the same principle that shaped Colby's journey with his mother. She, like him, intuitively holds a space where failure is feedback, not indictment. Where discomfort is guidance, not shame. Where vulnerability is welcomed, not weaponized. Where someone can be unfinished, unpolished, unsure—and still be deserving of dignity.

This is the exact environment our research uncovered in the 7 Conditions.

Safe Space is the condition where all the others weave together into a single lived environment.
It is where Purpose is remembered.
Where Commitment is reinforced.
Where Common Language is spoken.
Where Vulnerability breathes.
Where Consistency stabilizes.
Where Deep and Trusting Relationships form the container.

And within that container, people can:

- learn
- practice
- experiment
- fail
- adjust
- refine
- rise

Transformation is never born in comfort. And it is never sustained in fear.

Safe Space is the meeting point between both—the place where falling becomes feedback, pain becomes purpose, identity becomes grounded, and becoming finally becomes possible.

Safe Space as the Culmination of the 7 Conditions

In Groundwork—our leadership institute—we saw what happens when Safe Space becomes a lived reality, not a theory. Leaders from every corner of the community walked into our sessions carrying titles, reputations, responsibilities, political affiliations, and decades of habits. They represented government, business, nonprofits, education, law enforcement, faith communities—every background imaginable.

And yet, in that space, something rare happened:

They didn't just relate **professionally**.
They related **personally**.
They related **humanly**.

They shared failures.
They talked about doubts.
They pushed each other.
They grew together.

They became something more than colleagues—they became a community capable of transformation.

As children, we grow up with endless opportunities for practice. We rehearse instruments, we fall off skateboards, we try out for teams, we build forts, we fail at dance recitals, we paint sloppy pictures, we learn new languages, we try again and again. Childhood is filled with spaces designed **strictly for learning, failure, growth, and becoming.**

But somewhere along the way, adulthood convinces us that everything counts.
Everything must be perfect.
Mistakes are unacceptable.
Failure is fatal.
Doing it wrong is embarrassing.
Discomfort is avoided at all costs.

Adults forget how to practice.
Adults forget how to be beginners.
Adults forget how to become.

This is why the Safe Space condition matters so deeply.
Not just in theory.
Not just in teams.
But in **families, organizations, and entire communities.**

Groundwork showed us this at scale. High-level leaders—people who had not been "practiced with" in decades—finally had space to learn again. To struggle again. To experiment again. To be unpolished again. And their organizations changed because they changed. They took Safe Space back into their workplaces and replicated it—allowing their staff to fail forward, give honest feedback, name fears, surface conflict, take risks, and innovate.

We watched elected officials who had never spoken to each other before become genuine friends.
We watched CEOs cry in front of their competitors.
We watched nonprofit leaders who used to fight over funding share resources freely.
We watched leaders who once sabotaged each other end up apologizing and hugging with tears running down their cheeks.

Safe Space allowed them to practice becoming again, and that practice can lead to transformation.

The World We Live in Has Forgotten Safety

Let's be honest: we live in a world terrified of mistakes.

Families are organized around fear. Organizations are built around perfection. Communities are fractured by anger, resentment, isolation, and the belief that safety is impossible.

People walk through life armored.
Guarded.
Defensive.
Suspicious.
Searching for approval but afraid to be seen.

We have forgotten how to feel safe with one another.

This research is **not the answer**, but it is a necessary beginning.
These 7 Conditions are not scripture.
They are not the final word.

But they are a lens.
They are a framework.
They are a starting point for rediscovering what we have lost.

They are not everything—but they are enough to begin.

We need to rebuild a world where people can **become**.
Where families can practice truth and restoration.
Where teams can learn without fear.
Where organizations can innovate without punishment.
Where communities can heal and transform.

Becoming is the opposite of transaction.
It is not easy.
Please do not mistake it for that.

Start with **Purpose**.
Let it lead you into **Commitment**.
Let Commitment move you to **Common Language**.
Let Common Language open the door to **Vulnerability**.
Let Vulnerability create the ground for **Consistency**.
Let Consistency deepen into **Trusting Relationships**.
And those relationships—over time—will lead you right here:
To **Safe Space**.
To the environment where transformation finally becomes possible.

Safe Space Is Not Rest

Safe Space cannot be confused with *rest*. Rest—as adults often define it—is escape. Distraction. Stepping away. Taking a break from whatever is hard.

This is not that.

Rest, in a spiritual sense, is not the absence of effort. It is union with the Divine. It is taking on the yoke, not dropping it. It is doing *more*, not less—but doing it with God.

"We find rest," the Scripture teaches, "by taking His yoke upon us." Meaning we find rest **by engaging**, not retreating.

Good psychology echoes this:
You cannot heal by running from your problems.
You heal by facing them—supported.

Good philosophy echoes this:
Growth demands intention, tension, and repetition.

Even nature tells us this truth. In the Midwest plains, when monstrous storms sweep across the land, animals instinctively run away from them. Except the bison. The bison turn toward the storm and walk straight into it.

Why?

Because they know the fastest way out is through. Facing the storm shortens the suffering and strengthens the herd.

Likewise, becoming is not a retreat—it is an approach.

If we do not have Safe Spaces to learn, fail, practice, and become, then we become **ill-prepared** for life instead of *will*-prepared.

Transactional living feels like rest because it is easy—but it is an exhaustion disguised as comfort.

Transformation feels hard because it demands something of us—but it is a strengthening disguised as struggle.

Do not rest in transaction because transformation feels difficult. Rest in the safe spaces you intentionally create—for yourself and for others. Then run into transformation.

Exhausted, Not Rested

I want to live in such a way that when I kneel before my Maker one day, I am not "well-rested." I want to be exhausted—tired from running toward becoming, not away from it. Tired from creating Safe Space in my home, in my organization, in my community. Tired from facing storms head-on. Tired from helping others walk into their own storms with courage and dignity.

Colby's story is not one of comfort or ease.
It is not "safety" as the world defines it, some quiet cocoon where nothing hard can enter.
It is a story of holy discomfort.
Of courageous becoming.
Of choosing to break open instead of breaking apart.

His life is a masterclass in seeing everything—skateboarding, business, marriage, fatherhood, entrepreneurship—as a **vehicle for becoming**. His self-care is not indulgence; it is the care of the connection he holds with God, with himself, and with the people entrusted to him. His life reflects each of the 7 Conditions—not as a checklist, but as a lived philosophy.

And this is the invitation for all of us.

We become through purpose.
We stay the course through commitment.
We unite through common language.
We open through vulnerability.
We stabilize through consistency.
We deepen through trusting relationships.
And we transform through Safe Space.

Safe Space is not the end of the journey. It is the environment that makes the journey possible.

Reflection

Where in your life do you need to create a Safe Space for yourself to fail, practice, and grow?

____

____

____

Where do you need to turn toward the storm rather than away from it?

____

____

____

Who in your life needs you to create a Safe Space for them to become?

____

____

____

Which of the 7 Conditions feels least developed in you—and what is one step you can take to strengthen it?

____

____

____

____

Where have you been settling for transaction when you are called to transformation?

____

____

____

____

____

You do not become by accident. You become by intention. Safe Space is where that intention becomes alive.

Safe Space is where transformation becomes lived. It is where becoming takes root. It is where the cycle restarts.

Chapter *Twelve*:
TRANSFORMATION IS CAUGHT, NOT TAUGHT

When I set out to write this book—and honestly, when I began my research years ago—I was perplexed by one nagging tension:

How do you *teach* transformation when you fundamentally believe it cannot be taught?

It felt like an oxymoron. My experience, my research, and my own soul were all telling me the same thing: transformation is not something you download from a slide deck or absorb from a lecture. It is something you *catch*.

So, my question became, if transformation is caught, **how does that actually happen?** What are the conditions? What are the themes that keep showing up, and why?

I've wrestled with how to share these discoveries with the world without reducing them to formulas or checklists. My hope has never been to position myself as the "teacher" of transformation, but rather as a witness to it—a storyteller pointing to patterns I've seen again and again.

It may take a lifetime for me to understand the expanse of transformation fully, but that's a journey I am determined to remain on.

What I do know is this: just as my ancestors—and perhaps yours too—passed down wisdom through story, I have tried to do the same. My Filipino roots remind me of Pamana—the inheritance of those who came before us. Much of what I've shared in these pages is my attempt to honor that Pamana through stories of influence, purpose, vulnerability, failure, and becoming.

Stories were not listed as a formal "condition" in the research, but they were everywhere. Every participant in Groundwork shared stories—about their childhood, their pain, their breakthroughs, their failures, their relationships. When transformation showed up, it almost always came attached to a story.

Telling stories was one of our key strategies in the institute.

Capturing stories was another.

Human beings are storytellers. We are shaped by the stories we inherit and the stories we choose to tell. We share them informally in daily conversation, and formally in moments of influence, teaching, or leadership. This is not new. This is Indigenous. This is Pamana.

Which means *you* have had the ability to catalyze transformation this entire time through the development and sharing of your own story.

Each chapter, each reflection prompt, each example I've shared has been an invitation for you to uncover yours.

Truth be told, in reading this book, you have been part of an experiment.

You have not just been learning *about* transformation; you have been *walking through it.*

Now, I want you to go and share your story. Go and be a catalyst. Go and be an agent for real, lasting, deep change that moves you and others toward the positive potential of becoming more than you can imagine.

This is not cliché to me. This is literal. I believe you can do it. I believe it is possible.

Stop shaking hands.
Stop living purely transactional lives.
Share the breath of life now.

Do it with your ancestors—honor your Pamana. Do it with those you are building the future with—live in Kapwa. Do it by being fully present now—embody Unggno.

It starts with you.

Culture of One means it starts with the One. It has always been both the beginning and the end—the discovery and the unveiling.

These principles, Culture of One and the 7 Conditions—they work. They will catalyze transformation in your life, your organizations, and your communities. I have not only seen it through the stories in this book—I have lived it.

When the Conditions Became Personal

Many of the stories in this book included me but were not primarily my transformation stories. I was often the facilitator, the researcher, the observer, the one holding the space. Yes, I was deeply moved by the moment with my father in chapter six, and with Chad in chapter eight. Yes, chapters one through four show my initial discovery of Culture of One.

But now I want to share something different:

My **intentional journey** of taking these exact 7 Conditions and applying them in my own life—personally, and then professionally—to the highest level of exactness I could. I am still on that journey.

For a long time, I saw myself as somewhat of a third party to transformation in our leadership institute: the orchestrator of transformation in the community. I believed it. I felt it. I walked with those leaders and organizations. But I didn't fully internalize every principle the way I should have. Not like I did that day many years ago when I shook hands with that leader and realized how transactional I had become. I allowed the work of transformation I was doing to disguise the lack of transformation I was embodying—especially at home.

It took another extreme to wake me up. Again.

Let me take you to the moment when these conditions stopped being something I was studying and teaching and became something I could no longer avoid living.

Average at Home

I sat in my car outside the gym early one morning, reading Scripture and journaling as I had done for years. Rain poured outside. It was still dark. My wife sat in the passenger seat next to me. This had become our routine: she did her thing, I did mine, and we would often share our insights before heading into the gym.

On the surface, it was a good habit. But I didn't realize how transactional it had become.

At the time, I was finishing my PhD—two weeks removed from analyzing all of our data. The 7 Conditions had just emerged from the research. Groundwork was at its peak, working with leaders all over the community. It felt like the culmination of years of effort.

In my study that morning, I received what I felt was a revelatory insight about a problem I was facing at work. I was excited. I turned to my wife to share it.

Within seconds, that spiritual high turned into an argument about something that had happened a day or two earlier between us. I resisted. I argued back. In my head, I was thinking:

Why wouldn't she want to hear this insight? Look at what I've accomplished. I've built a leadership institute. I'm nearly done with a PhD. I've created financial stability for our family. Our kids' needs are met... you know the drill of psychological defense when arguing...

I defended myself—like many of us do when confronted by those we love.

It escalated to the point where she opened the door, stormed out into the rain, and walked into the gym without me.

I sat, frustrated and confused, thinking:

How can I be working so hard to be excellent in every outward area of my life, and this is what happens on a random morning in my car? How could I receive such a beautiful insight about work and be in an argument with my wife seconds later?

It's in moments like those that transformation can feel like a fluffy ideal—not something made for real life.

But as I sat there in my own self-pity, something shifted. I thought about the last ten-plus years: the discoveries, Culture of One, the fresh 7 Conditions. And a realization hit me hard:

In my pursuit of excellence at work—professionally, academically, in the community—I had become average at home.

Average as a husband. Average as a father. If I were honest, I would be considered average as a friend.

That dichotomy stung. It wrenched my heart wide open to the reality of my own imposter syndrome. I preached transformation all day, claimed to have "cracked the code," and yet there I sat—living transactionally in the most important relationships of my life. It was more painful than the realization of shaking hands with a leader I didn't like. I was metaphorically shaking hands in the most important relationship in my life... had I not learned anything?

For the next thirty minutes in that car, I sat there—first broken, then clear.

I knew I had the answers in front of me. I had a methodology. I had a framework. I had 7 Conditions and Culture of One staring back at me.

I left that moment with a new resolve:

If I was going to be excellent anywhere, I needed to be excellent **everywhere** that mattered most. Otherwise, what was the point?

It was another "running down the mountain" moment, just like the one I described earlier in the book. The difference this time was that I didn't just have a spiritual and emotional feeling—I had a structure.

So, I went to work.

Turning the Conditions Into Habits

I took the 7 Conditions one by one and turned them into habits.

PURPOSE

I already had a clear sense of purpose:

To give my heart to God by being an influence for good and catalyzing transformation in the world.

I thought about it often. I shared it with others. **But I lacked a daily practice to anchor it.**

I opened the notes app on my phone—where I had sporadically journaled before—and turned it into a daily ritual. I wrote my purpose at the top, along with my core values. I made a commitment: I would never miss a day of seeing or reading that purpose.

COMMITMENT

I reflected on what it means to *choose—and then keep choosing*. I wrote "becoming" goals for my life, not just outcome goals. I knew that to become those things, I would have to choose them on days I didn't feel like it.

COMMON LANGUAGE

I recommitted to the language I used with myself and my wife. I started collecting phrases and reminders that tethered me to who I wanted to be:

- "Stay faithful."
- "Do hard things."

- "Control what you can control."
- "Remember the Big Three."

Many of these came from Jason, as you read in chapter six. They became anchors. I recited them. I wrote them. I looked at them every day.

VULNERABILITY

I decided to tell the truth—always. To face my fears. To ensure that every day, in some way, I would offer vulnerability: in a conversation, an apology, an admission, or a risk. Foremost with my wife and kids, then with others in my life.

CONSISTENCY

"Do ordinary things with sacred intention" became my way of living. I changed how I studied, journaled, exercised, and even how I ate. I stopped treating these as disconnected tasks and started treating them as connected rituals.

I realized that goals without action are just wishes. So, I turned goals into habits. Habits into rhythms. Rhythms into identity.

DEEP AND TRUSTING RELATIONSHIPS

I looked at all my relationships and decided to stop hoping they'd deepen "on their own." Starting with my wife and kids, I became intentional:

- More focused conversations.
- Better questions.
- Weekly date nights with purpose, not just proximity.
- Individual rituals with each child so they felt seen, not just managed.

I began to be more intentional with people at work, too. I apologized where I needed to. I asked different questions. I listened more.

SAFE SPACE TO LEARN, PRACTICE, AND FAIL

Finally, I realized I needed safe spaces in my life where I could fail, learn, and grow—on purpose.

My relationship with Tay (from the previous chapter) became one of those spaces. Our regular check-ins—first weekly, then often daily—evolved into a sacred place where we could be honest, challenge each other, and become. I needed that space not only in my marriage but outside of it. Those relationships are invaluable.

None of this happened overnight. It unfolded over months. New habits formed, old patterns were confronted, and slowly my inner world changed.

Here are some of the things that followed.

What Changed

Life became clearer—who I am, where I came from, and where I'm going.

I reconnected with my ancestors, my Pamana. That led to the traditional tattoo I mentioned earlier—not an act of rebellion, but an act of remembrance. A way to carry those who came before me, whose names have been forgotten, but whose lives made mine possible.

I lost over thirty pounds in three months. I completely changed what I put into my body.

I started journaling **every day**—no misses.
I read Scripture **every day**—no misses.
I never missed a workout.

I became more intentional in how I listened to my wife and kids. I looked them in the eyes and told them I loved them—not passively, but consciously. Every day. Our relationships reached a depth I had never experienced before.

My wife felt new to me again—as if we were back in the early days of our relationship, but with more honesty and more resilience. We still disagreed. We still had arguments. But now they felt like part of the journey, not threats to it.

At work, we expanded. We began working with other groups and teams outside of the philanthropic partnership that started all this. With the philanthropist's encouragement, we branched off to reach other communities.

We formed a partnership with a large foundation in the Midwest to help them create similar efforts where they lived. We grew our team. Financially, things were better than they had ever been. Friendships deepened.

I began to feel the visceral, intentional power of **becoming**.

It was hard work—but the outcomes were undeniable.

Trials and errors were no longer meaningless. Every disagreement, setback, or difficult day started to carry weight and purpose. My life stopped feeling like separate compartments and began to feel like a continuous journey of transformation.

Transformational moments were no longer random or purely dependent on the grace of others or of God. They began flowing out of a new version of me—a version actively pursuing excellence after finally admitting I had become average.

In other words, I began pursuing transformation after fully recognizing my own transaction.

We can change. Always.

The answers are not outside of us. They are in us.

The conditions don't create transformation by themselves—but they create the **soil** where transformation can take root.

The Next Phase of the Experiment

Eventually, one of our largest clients—a foundation with nearly 3 million dollars in committed contracts—suddenly rescinded. Multiple internal dynamics on their side, and perhaps some of our imperfections on our side, led to the decision.

It happened in a single phone call.

The old Chris—the transactional Chris—would have been outraged. Defensive. Blaming. "How could they? Why would they? We've done everything they asked. This is unfair."

But this time, something was different.

I remembered my purpose.
I remembered my commitments.
I remembered my common language—"control what you can control."
I remembered vulnerability, the relationships we had built, the love we had for them.

I didn't resist. We had hard conversations. I pushed back appropriately. But the tone was different.

We ended in understanding rather than bitterness.

Practically, it still meant I had to let team members go, wind down the contract, and rethink our business model. That hurt. There was grief in that.

We still finished our commitments, including several more trips to their city and headquarters. In those final visits, we continued to share the vision of transformation, to share the breath of life, to practice Culture of One to the very end.

On our last visit, members of their executive team said goodbye with tears, wishing the story could have unfolded differently. We walked away without resentment, still holding deep respect and affection for them. I still value and love my relationship with them, and I'm encouraged by their ongoing efforts in their community.

What could have ended in anger and blame became—through the Conditions—a chapter in our becoming.

Months later, as we closed out other contracts, I woke up one morning with another realization—and frankly, a wild idea.

I had spent years walking alongside leaders across sectors. I'd sat at tables with elected officials working through leadership development, and I have walked with nonprofit leaders through every imaginable headache they face. I have spent time in schools with leaders, teachers, and advisors who work tirelessly to support children and families. I have worked with and advised law enforcement through difficult years like 2020. I have consulted businesses trying to continuously make a profit in an ever-changing social landscape and workforce. I have sat with every leader and front-line staff imaginable, listening, consulting, coaching, and supporting. It was a tremendous gift to me and to our discoveries. But there was one thing I hadn't done:

I had never truly sat in *their* chair.

Sitting in the Chair

I had not carried the full weight they carried.

My P&L statements were not in the millions.
My staff count was not in the hundreds.
I had not been responsible for a twenty-four-seven operation.
I had not made decisions about hiring, firing, budgets, and culture with that level of complexity and consequence.

I had led, but I had not led *that* way.

So, the "crazy" idea was born:

Maybe the next iteration of Groundwork—and my own transformation—was another "experiment" to further deepen our research.

Maybe I needed to go sit in the very seat I'd spent years advising: to become the kind of leader I had been walking beside and to see if these 7 Conditions truly held up in a complex, high-pressure organizational environment.

So, I did.

I put myself back into the job market. I was recruited into healthcare, specifically post-acute care—skilled nursing and rehabilitation. They were willing to license and train me and then put me in the CEO seat of a facility. It was an opportunity to sit at the helm of a highly complex organization and apply everything I'd learned.

We uprooted from our dream house, close friendships, and long-standing connections in Oregon and moved to a new state, a new city, a new life.

The building I inherited had been losing money consistently for over two years. It had only turned a profit three times, by accident—and only by a few thousand dollars each time. It was a true top-to-bottom turnaround project.

To give you a sense of scale: these facilities often generate close to a million dollars in revenue each month. They operate on twenty-four-seven staffing models, with fifty to a hundred-plus employees and extremely high operational expenses—margins are often thin. The CEO oversees all departments and operations:

- Finance
- Human Resources
- Marketing and Sales
- Business office and collections
- Nursing and therapy

- Food services
- Housekeeping and laundry
- Maintenance, transportation, and grounds
- Social services and activities

It is a highly regulated, highly complex, and very stressful industry.

The industry stands on three pillars:

1. **Financial** – Driving revenue and controlling costs. Increasing EBITDAR margins by balancing census, payer mix, labor hours, and operating expenses.

2. **Clinical** – Ensuring high-quality, compliant care through strong nursing leadership and regulatory adherence.

3. **Cultural** – The "feel" of the building. The morale. The way people treat each other.

Financial and clinical support systems abound in the industry. There are consultants, software platforms, scorecards, and endless training for those.

But culture?

Culture is often reduced to pizza parties, decorations, or themed weeks. It lives or dies based almost entirely on the leader.

This was the perfect environment to test the 7 Conditions at full scale and develop leaders, not just managers.

It was intimidating because the industry was new, but not unfamiliar. I had seen what it took to catalyze transformation in a community and dozens of different organizations as a trusted advisor, consultant, and trainer. Now I would apply those same principles inside one building, as *the* leader, fully responsible for an entire operation.

I did what I had learned to do personally: I turned the 7 Conditions into daily, weekly, and monthly organizational habits.

Applying the Conditions as the Leader in "The Chair"

PURPOSE

The facility had no clear vision statement. The culture was fractured. Fear and complacency lived side by side. Silos separated departments.

So, we started with Purpose.

I listened. I observed. I talked with department heads, CNAs, housekeepers, nurses, therapists, kitchen staff—everyone. We looked at where the building and staff had been, the good and the bad, and built something we wanted to become together. That became our shared and official vision statement:

"To be a place where every person matters—and every moment has meaning."

It wasn't just written by leadership. We involved employees from across the building. People, on their own accord, began hanging it on their own. Staff referenced it in huddles. We celebrated it. It became a guiding light that catalyzed everything else.

COMMITMENT

We instituted consistent oversight meetings and processes to keep key business areas top of mind. We didn't just have meetings—we honored them. We showed up. We stayed accountable to what we said we would do.

Choosing to be committed to all the systems, processes, and procedures—intentionally—became part of fulfilling our vision. None of the staff had ever taken the time to see how even the most granular, basic, or mundane tasks contributed to our vision. Our newfound commitment helped people see precisely how they belonged to something bigger.

COMMON LANGUAGE

I introduced the 7 Conditions themselves and the Rooted Framework from chapter seven. This gave us a shared language for:

- Discussing problems
- Naming dynamics
- Disagreeing without attacking
- Owning our part

Once people had language, they had leverage. This helped all our conversations to remind us about what we truly cared about, who we wanted to become, and how to work through problems. In this industry, problems and setbacks come in abundance. Having a common language provided clarity for defining, planning, and addressing these problems in an opportunistic way.

VULNERABILITY

I went first. I shared my fears, my mistakes, my learning curve as a newcomer to healthcare. Slowly, the leadership team began to open up too. Over time, people shared more openly about burnout, frustration, and hope—the stuff that usually stays under the surface.

Together, we faced the fears of past failures and overcame them in stride. There is no telling how much this impacted our ability to see incredible differences in not only our culture, but also the bottom line.

CONSISTENCY

We became consistent in our processes and in our interactions. We didn't nail it perfectly, but we kept showing up. The ordinary meetings, check-ins, and daily practices became sacred spaces where we chose intention over autopilot.

Once the team was able to see what worked and what turned our building around so quickly, they realized that doing the ordinary with intention changed their results and increased performance.

DEEP AND TRUSTING RELATIONSHIPS

We prioritized relationships. We opened communication lines between departments. We clarified roles and expectations. We had regular check-ins—not just about tasks, but about people. We made trust-building *part* of the work, not something "extra."

I focused on going deep in the areas where the building needed it most, instead of going wide. This helped people see and feel the importance of the *one* in the team.

SAFE SPACE TO LEARN, PRACTICE, AND FAIL

Slowly, the building became a place where people could speak up, try new approaches, and even fail—without being shamed. We still had standards and accountability. But people began to feel like they could bring their whole selves to work. Our culture, in just a few short months, became one of belonging and becoming. People started to work with excitement and hope when just months previously, for many of them, showing up for work was dreadful and the relationships were toxic.

None of this was smooth. The journey was full of setbacks, fear, stress, and long days. I am far from a perfect leader, and the team was not perfect either. There was still a lot more to improve upon.

But the results?

In just a few months, the building made an incredible turnaround.

We didn't fire our way to a new culture. I didn't bring in a new "dream team." I worked with what I had, the same team that had been there for years. The same team that had been **losing** $50,000 to $200,000 a month became the team that turned the building around.

Within the first thirty days, we saw nearly a 200 percent swing in net income—from negative $60,000 to positive $50,000. Each month after that, it continued to improve.

Turnover decreased by over 50 percent. Key operational expenses also dropped by over 50 percent. The environment changed—people smiled more, laughed, and collaborated. Patients and families noticed the difference. I remember one moment when I was pushing a resident in her wheelchair to lunch. She saw our vision statement on the wall and asked me to stop. Looking at it with her eighty seven years of life and wisdom, she then said to me.

"I am happy to be in a place where that is what you believe. I feel it."

On another occasion, a housekeeper who had spent nearly twenty years doing janitorial work—often unseen and treated as a means to an end— stopped me in the hallway and said,

"Chris, I need to tell you something. I have been doing this work for a long time, but I have never been excited to show up to work like I have here. You asked me the other day what my purpose was at the all-staff meeting... no one has ever asked me that. Thank you. I have never considered it. I'm going to start knowing how to answer that question."

He told me a few days later that he now defined his purpose as working hard for his family and making people smile every day.

Beautiful moments started peppering in every day, every week. The building that once operated in fear, silos, and transactional repetition became a hub for the transformation of its people.

This was just one building.

I later ran another, in a different state, with even more complex cultural and financial challenges—and saw similar results. Accountability increased. Communication improved. Our EBITDAR margin went from 18 percent when I arrived to 30 percent when I left.

Again, I don't share these numbers to boast. I share them to emphasize this:

Everything that truly moved the needle did **not** come from industry training.

It came from intentionally applying the 7 Conditions.

A Harsh Reality About Transformation

It is worth noting that current research suggests more than **70 percent of organizational transformation efforts fail**. Additionally, over **75 percent of leadership development programs and trainings are deemed ineffective**. There is a clear correlation here: organizations cannot transform without leaders who are themselves transformative. And if most leadership development efforts fall short, it means the majority of leaders never actually learn how to create meaningful change—let alone transformational change.

These numbers represent only the organizations formally studied. My assumption?
The real failure rate is even higher.
And the true success rate—for deep, sustained transformation—is
even lower.

All of this to say: the work of transformation is not just difficult in theory—it is difficult in reality. **Seven to eight out of ten leaders will fail to lead transformative change.** And **seven to eight out of ten organizations** attempting transformation will not succeed.

This is the landscape I stepped into.

Most new administrators who inherit buildings with the kind of losses I have shared do not turn them around that quickly; some never do. It can happen with highly seasoned leaders, but even with years of experience, the failure rate remains high. The companies that have found long-term success in healthcare have figured out how to develop strong, consistent leaders capable of building strong cultures. Two prominent companies that have excelled at this are Ensign Services and Plum Healthcare.

So why did it happen for me so quickly?

Because I applied the **7 Conditions of Transformation**:

1. Purpose

2. Commitment

3. Common Language

4. Vulnerability

5. Consistency

6. Deep and Trusting Relationships

7. Safe Space to Learn, Practice, and Fail

Day in and day out, I focused on living Culture of One and creating the conditions where transformation could be caught.

It was hard. My second building was in another state, away from my family. None of it was easy, and there are many more stories I could tell from that season.

But I wanted you to see something concrete:

Someone like me—who had never run a large organization or overseen such a complex operation—could step into the CEO role and see rapid, meaningful results. Not because I was the smartest person in the room or the most experienced in the industry—I most certainly was neither of those. But because I had learned how to transform culture.

Eventually, I felt called back—to *this* work. Back to supporting leaders across sectors, back to communities, developing leaders at scale, back to this book.

I realized something important:

Transformation is not compartmentalized.

When you're on the journey, it affects everything—family, work, health, purpose, community. It is not just something you *do* for a living. It becomes how you live.

Finally, the Transformation in Our Community

The entirety of this book has followed the arch line of the leadership cohorts we launched because of the work I did with a philanthropist many years ago. I've shared examples in every chapter about the remarkable things that happened along the way. Still, I want to make sure the evidence is highlighted through clear data points—just as I've shared measurable data points from my own transformation.

These conditions were created within the institute at first—an experiment, an unfolding, a discovery of what worked. Eventually, they evolved into critical anchor points we intentionally implemented every single year, month after month, throughout our entire program.

PURPOSE

Purpose was everything from the moment we vetted leaders. Applications were open to the public, but the majority came from nominations by previous cohort members—our alumni. Each year, they personally nominated one to three leaders, sharing the vision of Groundwork with them and inviting them to become catalysts for transformation in our community.

Because of that peer-driven process, leaders came into their initial interviews already familiar with our purpose. In the interview itself, the **first** thing we discussed was the history and purpose of the entire initiative—where we came from and who we wanted to become together.

We revisited this **every single month**. Purpose became a consistent thread in our conversations and dialogue. We watched it shift from idealistic in the first months to deeply embodied around month four or five, when leaders began to "get it."

During our first month, we took cohorts to the coast for a launch retreat. We spent an entire day on purpose—not just Groundwork's institutional purpose, but their own. Leaders defined their "why" in twenty words or less. Around month four or five, these individual purposes began to take on life. They expanded beyond the self and became part of a shared **Culture of One**.

Purpose was the beginning and the end of our programming. It was foundational.

COMMITMENT

Commitment was a lesson we learned the hard way. Early on, leaders were committed "in spirit," but not always in body. Attendance wasn't 100 percent, but in a transformational leadership institute—where we met only once a month—attendance was critical. Their commitment to our purpose had to extend into their habits, their participation, their "homework," their group work, and everything the program required.

In one of our early years, a session that began with all twenty five leaders ended with only six remaining—*and the day wasn't even halfway over*. That moment taught us that commitment needed to be non-negotiable long before we realized it would become one of the 7 Conditions.

So we created a thorough commitment process during the interview. Because the institute was fully philanthropic—free to participants investing roughly **$20,000 into each leader per year**—we told them that number. We shared our commitment to them and then asked them to commit to us. Right there in the interview, if they accepted, they signed a letter of commitment stating that—outside of absolute emergencies—they would fully participate, even when it was difficult.

This commitment became a shared standard throughout the year. Cohort members held each other accountable. CEOs, founders, administrators, elected officials—no matter their status—knew what they had agreed to. If someone came late or left early, the rest of the group knew the commitment they had made together. Commitment became natural. Necessary. A condition for transformation.

COMMON LANGUAGE

If one condition was intentionally built from the very beginning, it was **common language**.

Before Groundwork existed, Jason, Salam, and I were already talking about the need for a shared language rooted in curriculum. We initially used content from other sources, but quickly realized it wasn't holistic and didn't address the real problem we were trying to solve—the problem of **transaction.**

I went to work. With the support of an incredible team, I created the **Rooted Framework**, which I described in the chapter on common language: *choose words that remind you who you are.* The framework improved every year and became the program's handbook—the lynchpin for practical conversations and the application of principles.

The Rooted Framework drove community dialogue, individual goal-setting, and group work. Diagrams, charts, activities—everything pointed leaders back to the same soil, seeds, weeds, and fruit.

In addition, we curated mantras, readings, guest speakers, and alumni panels. But everything flowed back to that common language. It tethered the work. It gave leaders not just the **why**, but the **how**.

I cannot overstate how important this common language was in the process.

VULNERABILITY

As shared in the vulnerability chapter, this was one of our highest-rated research findings. But vulnerability wasn't initially intentional.

It began with storytelling—inviting leaders to go deep and get uncomfortable. But simply "asking" wasn't enough. People naturally keep the door shut that fear tells them to keep closed. So, we built intentional activities, shared videos, and offered vulnerability from our team first. Slowly, the soil softened.

Leaders began taking risks, opening up, getting vulnerable. Our sessions became laboratories for the strength that vulnerability creates. Many of our most transformational moments occurred *right on the other side of vulnerability*.

We soon realized it wasn't just an element of transformation—it was a condition of it.

CONSISTENCY

Like common language, the idea of consistency was intentional from the outset. We didn't yet know it would be one of the 7 Conditions, but we knew consistency would be essential.

Leaders across sectors can build relationships and "catch" transformation—but it takes time. A three-week retreat might have done similar things, but no one had the time for that. And even the monthly cadence was a sacrifice. Yet we knew consistency mattered—not only in the macro (showing up each month) but in the micro: raising hands, sharing thoughts, asking questions, participating with intention.

Because we were clear on purpose, everything we did carried meaning. Consistency became part of their identity as a group. It became a quiet war cry:

"We must be consistent. We must show up. We must be vulnerable and lead. If not us, then who?"

Doing ordinary things with sacred intention became a hallmark of every cohort.

DEEP AND TRUSTING RELATIONSHIPS

Most programs talk about relationship-building, but few move beyond the superficial. In fact, increasing cross-sector relationships was one of my original goals when Groundwork began. But those early relationships remained surface deep.

Culture of One and the 7 Conditions revealed why: trust wasn't built because the relationships lacked the foundation the conditions provide.

We knew that deep relationships required clear purpose, commitment, common language, vulnerability, and consistency. As outlined in the relationships chapter, trust was an **outcome** of everything that preceded it.

One insight came from a police chief in one of our early cohorts. He told us he used to attend luncheons and community gatherings without realizing how transactional they were. One night at a formal dinner—with spouses invited—he introduced his wife to a nonprofit leader he worked closely with. That leader's demeanor conveyed disinterest—not in him, but in his wife. The chief realized he felt the same way about the other leader's spouse. In that instant, the superficiality of their "relationship" became glaringly obvious.

At Groundwork, we intentionally went deep—not in a pushy or inappropriate way, but in an authentic and human way. After vulnerability, this was the **second-highest data point** in our research. No surprise.

SAFE SPACE TO LEARN, PRACTICE, AND FAIL

Finally: safe space. This condition emerged unintentionally at first; we didn't fully know in what would form when we invested so deeply in leaders. But within the first cohort, the space became a haven—not just psychologically safe, but emotionally and relationally safe.

Leadership can be lonely. Leaders often cannot share their deepest struggles with staff, stakeholders, or even family. But in Groundwork, they found people who understood them. They found people carrying similar burdens. This space allowed them to challenge each other, support each other, and grow together with deep respect and love.

One year, a large foundation from across the country joined several of our sessions as they were interested in attempting a similar venture in their own community. Their first experience was our end-of-year banquet—a formal event where alumni and current leaders attended with a plus-one. It was elegant—speaker, dinner, formal attire—but the atmosphere was unlike typical formal gatherings. It was vulnerable, real, and authentic. Visceral. These foundation leaders could not believe what they were witnessing—a room of cross-sector leaders creating an environment of belonging and becoming at this level. They told us, "We simply cannot see how this would be possible in our own community." We assured them that it takes time, but it is possible. That foundation, after a partnership with us, has since built a similar program.

This final condition—Safe Space—became the capstone of the 7 Conditions. It showed us that the impossible was, in fact, possible.

By the Numbers

Groundwork Leadership cohorts have shown that when the 7 Conditions are intentionally practiced, transformation doesn't just happen—it compounds.

Across multiple years, cohorts, and hundreds of leaders:

- **100 percent of leaders set and accomplished meaningful goals** aligned with personal growth and every condition of transformation.

- **90 percent of leaders made fundamental internal changes—** clarifying values, strengthening identity, and shifting behaviors.

- **96 percent of leaders reported increased confidence,** better decision-making, and a stronger sense of being equipped to create lasting change.

- **Community engagement increased by 90 percent,** with leaders reporting a higher desire to contribute beyond the workplace.

- **Belief in the community's capacity to grow increased by 75 percent**, demonstrating how individual transformation radiates outward.

These aren't abstract principles. They work—measurably and repeatedly. Groundwork Leadership wasn't just a program. It became a catalyst for personal, organizational, and community transformation.

My Hope for You

Stop shaking hands.

Not literally (unless that's the right symbol for you), but certainly metaphorically."

Break out of transaction. Share the breath of life.

Reflect on your past—your Pamana. Build a future with those you are connected to—your Kapwa. Be fully present with those in front of you now—your Unggno.

Apply the 7 Conditions in your life, your organizations, and your communities. In the postface, I share tools to help you get started practically—but you don't need to wait for that.

Just start.

Keep the journey you began in this book going. Don't stop. Reflection is your superpower.

- Start with your **Purpose**.
- Live a life of **Commitment** to it.
- Discover the **Common Language** that keeps you tethered to your values.
- Be **Vulnerable**—face your fears and tell the truth.
- Be **Consistent**—never miss a day of showing up with intention.
- Go **Deep** in your relationships—build trust that can withstand any storm.

- And create **Safe Spaces** where you and others can learn, practice, fail, and become.

Transformation is not taught.
It is caught.

You cannot control transformation itself.
But you can control the conditions.

That part is on you.

I beckon you to be philanthropic—not just with money, but with your life. Give more. Do more. Lift more.

This all started with a philanthropic journey and a pure desire for transformation, sitting knee to knee with a man who would forever change my life. I believe that is the only way it can live on—through you, through your organizations, through your families, through your communities. Imagine me, now, sitting knee to knee with you, offering a valuable resource—these 7 Conditions and Culture of One. What will you do to make a difference in your life and world?

You are enough right now. But we have work to do.
Be the One.

ACKNOWLEDGMENTS

No work of transformation is ever done alone.

This book belongs to leaders everywhere who long to build something deeper than performance. To philanthropists who push beyond comfort in service of their communities. To families and neighborhoods navigating darkness and confusion—may these pages offer even the smallest glimmer of light toward what is still possible. The ideas in this book were not born in isolation; they were forged in real rooms, with real people, facing real complexity.

I am deeply grateful to the communities who allowed me to learn alongside them—especially the leaders and people of Salem, Oregon, a home away from home. Your humility, courage, and commitment shaped not only this framework but my own becoming. The work of Groundwork Leadership served as a living laboratory for what these pages describe. To the leaders and people of Salem I had the privilege to work with—you are the quiet catalysts of transformation. So many names come to mind, but some who have deeply impressed upon my heart are: Anthony, Kim, Tony, Hassan, Evann, Bubba, Kevin, Jared, Rhonda, Zack, Sue, Carlos, Troy, Alison, Rachel, Steve, Kanoe, Travez, Rick, Mark, Jordan, Ryan, Scott, Artonya, Jim, and Jasmine. Stay humble. Stay committed. Stay vulnerable. The ripples you create will become waves.

To the mentors who believed in me long before I saw clearly myself—thank you. JT, you modeled how to order life rightly: God first, family second, children third. You taught me that leadership without integrity is hollow. LT, your generosity changed the trajectory of my life and will echo through generations. Salam Noor, you walked with me through the highs and lows of scholarship and leadership alike; your brotherhood has been a gift. Dr. Natalie Hamrick and the faculty who guided my academic journey, thank you for sharpening my thinking with both rigor and grace.

To Seamus Fitzgerald, Kim Makekau, Michael Liga Liga, and David Whippy. You all were examples to me of individuals who loved your faith, family, and culture. Teaching me that my Asia-Pacific heritage can be more than just where my father is from—but within my that very culture I can find identity, mana (power), and the ability to influence others for good.

To my coaches and teammates throughout my athletic journey—thank you. As a collegiate athlete and lifelong member of teams, I learned lessons no classroom could teach: hard work, grit, loyalty, how to lose with dignity, and how to win with humility. To my teammates who shaped me in those formative years—Colby, Landon, Scott, Bent, and Abe—you pushed me beyond what I believed I was capable of. And to my coach, Mark Davis, thank you for demanding excellence while modeling character. The discipline and brotherhood forged on fields, in training rooms, in team rooms, and on long plane/bus rides became part of the foundation upon which this work now stands. I am grateful to have walked that road with each of you.

To my parents—Senen (Bong) and Barbara Pineda—Mom and Dad. You gave me life, heritage, and identity. From my mother's lineage across England, Scandinavia, and Germany, and from my father's Filipino and Austronesian roots, I carry the sacrifices of generations. To my in-laws, Mike and Stephanie, thank you for raising a daughter whose strength, kindness, and faith have shaped me more than you know.

To my ancestors—known and unknown—I carry your Pamana. To those whose names were erased through colonization, whose language and practices were pressed down but not extinguished, I honor you. I will continue to search for you. I respectfully offer "Mano Po" across time, grateful for the identity you preserved so that I might live it forward.

To my children—Eva, Mateo, and Tala—you are among my greatest motivations. You may not yet understand the long nights or the sacrifices, but I hope one day you will see that this work was never about achievement; it was about becoming the kind of father worthy of you.

While this is not a religious book, I must, above all, give gratitude to the Lord my God and to His Son, Jesus Christ. In moments of uncertainty,

You have been my rock. In moments of loss, my light. All that I am, and all that I hope to become, rests in You.

And finally—to my wife, Makenzie.

This book would not exist without you.

You have believed in me when clarity felt distant. You have carried our family when my work required more than it should have. You have endured relocations, risk, uncertainty, and sacrifice with a steadiness that humbles me. Long before this research began, you were shaping the conditions in our home and life—purpose, commitment, language, vulnerability, consistency, trust—often without recognition.

Every milestone in my life traces back to your quiet faith and love. Your belief in me began when we were young and has carried us through multiple careers, graduate degrees, three children, and years of study. You have reminded me who I am when I have forgotten. You have called me upward when I have grown tired. Your love is a living expression of the very transformation this book describes.

If these ideas endure, it is because you endured with me.

This is only the beginning.

ABOUT THE AUTHOR

Dr. Chris Pineda is a leadership strategist, researcher, speaker, and founder of Groundwork Leadership. A Filipino-American raised between cultures, his work is deeply shaped by Asia-Pacific Indigenous wisdom and its enduring emphasis on community, identity, and relational depth. With a PhD in organizational psychology and over a decade of cross-sector experience spanning philanthropy, healthcare, executive leadership, and community development, his work centers on one enduring question: what truly catalyzes lasting transformation—in individuals and in systems?

Through years of doctoral research, field testing, and real-world application, Chris developed the 7 Conditions of Transformation™—a framework grounded in both modern psychology and Indigenous principles that have shaped Pacific cultures for generations. His work bridges ancestral insight and organizational science, helping leaders and communities move from transactional survival to transformational growth.

Chris has facilitated hundreds of workshops, coached senior executives and founders, led cultural and operational turnarounds, and designed leadership initiatives across sectors. His passion for Asia-Pacific worldviews—including concepts such as Pamana (lineage/legacy), Kapwa (shared identity), and relational responsibility—continues to inform how he teaches, designs, and leads.

Whether working with executives, families, nonprofits, or community leaders, his approach remains the same: transformation is not forced—it is invited through the conditions we intentionally create.

He lives with his wife and children, committed to honoring his heritage and practicing the principles he teaches.

WORK CITED

Arbinger Institute. (2010). *Leadership and self-deception: Getting out of the box* (2nd ed.). Berrett-Koehler.

Bandura, A. 1997. *Self-Efficacy: The Exercise Of Control.* W. H. Freeman.

Buber, M. 1970. *I and Thou* (W. Kaufmann, Trans.). Scribner. (Original work published 1923)

Cacioppo, J. T., and Patrick, W. 2008. *Loneliness: Human Nature and the Need for Social Connection.* W. W. Norton.

Deci, E. L., and Ryan, R. M. 2000. "The "What" and "Why" of Goal Pursuits: Human Needs and the Self-Determination of Behavior." *Psychological Inquiry*, no. 11, 4: 227–268.

Dweck, C. S. 2006. *Mindset: The New Psychology of Success.* Random House.

Edmondson, A. C. 2019. *The Fearless Organization: Creating Psychological Safety in the Workplace for Learning, Innovation, and Growth.* Wiley.

Fiorina is credited with saying, "Courage is not the absence of fear, courage is acting in spite of fear." (Quotefancy, n.d.)

Enriquez, V. G. 1992. *From Colonial to Liberation Psychology: The Philippine Experience.* University of the Philippines Press.

Fredrickson, B. L. 2001. "The role of positive emotions in positive psychology." *American Psychologist*, no. 56, 3: 218–226.

Frankl, V. E. 2006. *Man's Search for Meaning.* Beacon Press. (Original work published 1946)

Ford, C. 2020. *Dangerous Love: Transforming Fear and Conflict at Home, at Work, and in the World.* Berrett-Koehler.

Hau'ofa, E. 1994. Our Sea of Islands. *The Contemporary Pacific,* no. 6, 1: 147–161.

Hughes, M. 2011. "Do 70 Percent of All Organisational Change Initiatives Really Fail? *Journal of Change Management.*"

Jocano, F. L. 1997. *Filipino Value System: A Cultural Definition.* Punlad Research House.

Jones-Schenk, J. 2019. "70% Failure Rate: An Imperative for Better Change Management." *Journal for Continuing Education in Nursing,* no. 50, 4: 148–149.

Kegan, R., and Lahey, L. L. 2009. *Immunity to Change: How to Overcome It and Unlock Potential in Yourself and Your Organization.* Harvard Business Press.

Laloux, F. 2014. *Reinventing Organizations: A Guide to Creating Organizations Inspired by the Next Stage of Human Consciousness.* Nelson Parker.

Lederach, J. P. 2005. *The Moral Imagination: The Art And Soul of Building Peace.* Oxford University Press.

McKinsey & Company. 2021, December 7. *Successful Transformations Still Leave Value on the Table.* McKinsey & Company.

Palmer, P. J. 1998. *The Courage to Teach: Exploring the Inner Landscape of a Teacher's Life.* Jossey-Bass.

Pineda, Chris. 2024. "Understanding Leaders' Experiences of a Leadership Institute: A Combination of Transformational Leadership, Cross-Sector Collaboration, and Charitable Foundations as Catalysts." *Doctoral Dissertations and Projects.* 5176.

Ryan, R. M., and Deci, E. L. 2017. *Self-Determination Theory: Basic Psychological Needs in Motivation, Development, and Wellness.* Guilford Press.

Schein, E. H. 2010. *Organizational Culture and Leadership* (4th ed.). Jossey-Bass.

Schutz, A. 1967. *The Phenomenology of the Social World.* Northwestern University Press.

Seligman, M. E. P. 2011. *Flourish: A Visionary New Understanding of Happiness and Well-Being.* Free Press.

Senge, P. M. 2006. *The Fifth Discipline: The Art and Practice of the Learning Organization* (Rev. ed.). Doubleday. (Original work published 1990)

Siegel, D. J. 2010. *The Mindful Therapist.* W. W. Norton.

Stanner, W. E. H. 2009. *The Dreaming and Other Essays.* Black Inc.

Warner, C. T. 2001. *Bonds That Make Us Free: Healing Our Relationships, Coming to Ourselves.* Shadow Mountain.

Wilcken, L. 2010. *Filipino Tattoos: Ancient to Modern.* Tuttle Publishing.

GLOSSARY OF INDIGENOUS TERMS
(WITH CITATIONS)

Pamana

Definition: Legacy, inheritance, or lineage—spiritual, cultural, relational, and ancestral. **Notes:** Central to Filipino Indigenous psychology as an understanding that one's identity emerges from ancestors and past generations.
Cited in: Wilcken. 2010; Jocano. 1997

Kapwa

Definition: "Shared Identity"; the understanding that *I am who I am because we are*. Relationship is not peripheral—relationship **is identity**.
Cited in: Enriquez. 1992

Unggno / Unggno (Ilocano)

Definition: Shared breath; the spiritual, relational act of "breathing life together." Represents presence, relational attunement, and the fire of connection.
Cited in: Ilocano linguistic/anthropological roots; Wilcken (2010) discusses related breath/mana concepts.

Vā / Vā (Samoan)

Definition: The sacred relational space between people; not empty, but alive. Must be tended, protected, and nurtured.
Cited in: Tamasese and Polynesian scholarship; Hau'ofa (1994) connects to Oceania relational space.

Tauhi Vā (Tongan)

Definition: The disciplined practice of **nurturing, honoring, and caring for** the space between people. **Cited in:** Tongan Relational Ethics Literature (Ka'ili scholarship).

Whanaungatanga (Māori)

Definition: Kinship, deep relational belonging, collective identity, and mutual responsibility.
Cited in: Māori sociocultural literature (Stanner, 2009, provides Indigenous relational worldview parallels.)

Manaakitanga (Māori)

Definition: Hospitality, generosity, and uplifting others; the ethic of honoring another's dignity through care.
Cited in: Māori cultural texts; aligns with relational dignity frameworks.

Batok (Filipino tattooing; from chapter five)

Definition: Traditional hand-tapped Filipino tattooing, connected to lineage, identity, courage, and rites of passage.
Cited in: Wilcken. 2010

Pākū (Filipino; tattoo-specific)

Definition: "To strike" or "to tap"—describing the rhythmic technique of hand-tapped tattooing.
Cited in: Wilcken. 2010

Anitu (Filipino Indigenous belief)

Definition: Ancestral spirits or guardians; tied into Pamana and Indigenous cosmologies.
Cited in: Wilcken. 2010

Lifeblood Concepts (Pacific)

Mana (Polynesian), Breath, Spirit, Life-force

These were referenced conceptually in my writing through Unggno and shared breath practices. **Cited in:** Hau'ofa. 1994; Stanner. 2009; Polynesian anthropological sources.

WORK WITH CHRIS

BRINGING THE 7 CONDITIONS
TO LIFE AND LEADERSHIP

The 7 Conditions of Transformation are not just ideas—they are design principles. When intentionally applied, they reshape how individuals live and how organizations operate.

Dr. Chris Pineda partners with individuals, leaders, and organizations to create environments where transformation is not accidental—but sustainable.

Transformation can begin in a single life.
It can also reshape an entire culture.

LIFE

Personal Growth and Family Transformation
Transformation begins at home—within identity, relationships, and daily habits. The same 7 Conditions that strengthen organizations also deepen marriages, families, and individual purpose.

Offerings Include:

Keynote and Community Talks
Purpose-driven messages for churches, universities, nonprofits, and community gatherings focused on identity, becoming, and relational depth.

Personal Transformation Workshops
Interactive sessions designed to help individuals clarify purpose, strengthen commitment, build relational depth, and align daily behavior with long-term becoming.

Family and Relationship Intensives
Framework-based experiences that help families develop shared language, rebuild trust, and create safe environments for growth.

Individual Coaching
One-on-one coaching for leaders, entrepreneurs, parents, and individuals seeking clarity, alignment, and intentional growth. Transformation at the personal level changes generations. What is chosen today shapes tomorrow.

LEADERSHIP

Organizational Culture and Executive Development
Sustainable performance is built on relational depth—not just strategy. The 7 Conditions provide a framework for leaders seeking more than surface-level change.

Offerings Include:

Keynote Speaking
Research-grounded, culturally rooted presentations that challenge transactional leadership and equip audiences with a clear pathway toward transformation.

Organizational Assessments
Diagnostic tools aligned with the 7 Conditions to identify cultural gaps and opportunities for deeper alignment.

Leadership and Culture Design
Strategic facilitation, executive off-sites, and implementation plans to embed purpose, commitment, shared language, and trust into daily operations.

Coaching and Implementation
Focused coaching for executives, founders, and senior leaders navigating complexity, growth, and cultural change.

Transformation is not achieved through policies alone.
It is built through conditions intentionally designed and consistently practic

BOOK CHRIS PINEDA
TO SPEAK WITH YOUR TEAM, PROGRAM, OR ORGANIZATION

Whether in a family, a nonprofit, a corporation, or a community—the work is the same:

Choose purpose. Commit daily.
Build shared language. Lead with depth.
Transformation is not forced. It is invited.

To inquire about speaking, consulting, or partnership:
chrispineda.me and groundworkleadership.org
chris@groundworkleadership.org

Representing a community of authors whose books have collectively sold hundreds of millions of copies, the founders of The Gray + Miller Agency launched Maison Vero, a professional publishing house that partners with rising authors to bring their thought leadership to the world. Our representation covers every aspect of thought leadership, including U.S. senators, governors, and ambassadors, billionaire founders and entrepreneurs, researchers, academics, scientists, consultants, practitioners, social influencers, C-suite leaders, adventurers, professional athletes, artists, and creators. We partner with thought leaders and world changers like you who have a story to tell. By bringing decades of professional expertise to our clients, we are charting a new path in a timeless industry that transcends publishing norms, transforming powerful thoughts into impactful books that inspire minds, ignite hearts, and open doors.

Visit maisonvero.com to view our growing list of authors, or to submit a proposal for publication consideration.

Follow Maison Vero for insight and inspiration on social media:

 MaisonVero  MaisonVero  MaisonVeroPublishing

For information about special discounts for bulk purchases, please call 1-949-333-4872 or email info@graymilleragency.com.

Maison Vero is a partner brand of The Gray + Miller Agency, a speaking, literary, and talent consortium. For more information on the talent represented by The Gray + Miller Agency, or to bring any of our thought leaders to your organization or live event, please visit our website at **graymilleragency.com**.